# BOB DYLAN

## FOR GUITAR TAB

Compiled by Nick Crispin.
Edited by Adrian Hopkins.
Music arranged by Matt Cowe and Arthur Dick.
Music processed by Paul Ewers Music Design.
Cover design by Tim Field.
Cover photograph courtesy Getty.

Order No. AM995060
Printed in the UK.

ISBN: 978-1-84772-677-3

Visit Hal Leonard Online at
**www.halleonard.com**

Contact us:
**Hal Leonard**
7777 West Bluemound Road
Milwaukee, WI 53213
Email: info@halleonard.com

In Europe, contact:
**Hal Leonard Europe Limited**
42 Wigmore Street
Marylebone, London, W1U 2RY
Email: info@halleonardeurope.com

In Australia, contact:
**Hal Leonard Australia Pty. Ltd.**
4 Lentara Court
Cheltenham, Victoria, 3192 Australia
Email: info@halleonard.com.au

# FOREWORD
## BY PETER DOGGETT

In the early 1960s, when the likes of Peter, Paul & Mary and The Byrds were forging careers out of their interpretations of Bob Dylan's songs, his record company began to market his own albums with the rather plaintive but, as it turned out, stunningly perceptive line: 'No One Sings Dylan Like Dylan'.

They might have added, with equal accuracy, that nobody else plays guitar like Bob Dylan. Generations of budding musicians have been encouraged to pick up the instrument for the first time after hearing his records, fooled into believing that the apparent simplicity of his songs – often built around a handful of familiar chords, in accessible keys – would enable them to reproduce Dylan's style. Careful attention to his records, however, reveals that there is no such thing as 'the Bob Dylan guitar style', as his work combines many different and often starkly personal approaches to the instrument.

His guitar playing borrows from a variety of sources, from every American genre and beyond, encompassing the rhythmic strum of major and minor chords, delicate finger-picking, flat-picked blues licks, diminished or augmented jazz shapes, or more often an instinctive, free-flowing amalgam of all these techniques and more. It's the sum of a musical talent that endlessly displays the value of listening to and learning from your peers and predecessors. Elements of everyone whose music has touched Dylan's imagination – from Woody Guthrie to Robert Johnson, Willie Nelson to Jerry Garcia – are evident in the way he approaches his guitar.

Hence the value of these transcriptions, which unpick the musical tapestry of some of Dylan's most enduring songs, as they were originally recorded. That final qualification is vital: the persistent lesson of Dylan's career is that a recording is not a prototype that will be replicated on concert stages for decades to come, but merely the documentation of a moment in history. Heard a few minutes earlier or later, those familiar chord changes, riffs and runs might – indeed, almost certainly would – have been different. It's been a regular taunt of Dylan's critics that his live performances don't sound like the records, as if that were some kind of crime. The release of alternate takes of many Dylan masterpieces reveals that the process of transformation begins even as the records are being made. Take 'You're A Big Girl Now' and 'If You See Her, Say Hello', for example: as issued on the *Blood On The Tracks* album, both songs were performed in standard tuning. Yet a few weeks earlier, when assembling the original, withdrawn version of that album, Dylan had played both in open tuning: the same songs, but different chord shapes, a different feel, starkly different performances. And that creative reinvention continues every time that Dylan faces an audience, with the result that – to pluck another random example from the multitude of possibilities – the simple D major to C major change in the opening line of 'It Ain't Me, Babe' in 1964 had become an E minor to D minor shift eleven years later on the Rolling Thunder Tour.

Like all the aspects of his creativity, Dylan's musicianship is not written in stone but in flux. You can glimpse his refusal to paint safely between the lines in the performances that were captured for posterity on his records, and have now been transcribed for this collection. They range from his pioneering 1963 album *The Freewheelin' Bob Dylan* (arguably the most influential folk record in history) to modern masterpieces such as 'Blind Willie McTell' and 'Mississippi'.

Having established a pattern or a riff, and determined that it is hardy enough to support his song, he invariably toys with it, stretches with it, tests its ability to function within an infinite series of variations. Like his voice, which uncovers its own rhythm within the confines of a song, his guitar style is all about movement: it keeps the music on its toes, and its audience on a knife-edge of discovery. Yet that knack of driving forward a performance is only one facet of Dylan's command of movement. In an almost metaphysical way, his music – and his guitar-playing can epitomise this – is in a constant state of mutation, of evolution, of slipping the bounds of convention and inventing anew the world in which it is operating.

So these transcriptions invite you to retrace Dylan's steps and then – if you want to follow his example – remould them in your own image. Yet they also offer valuable insights into his talent and reveal some of the tricks of his craftsmanship: his willingness to use alternate tunings (the tuning of the original 'One Too Many Mornings' is a beauty); his delight in lowering his 6th string a couple of steps into a drop-D tuning; and his unashamed use of the capo to deliver exactly the musical effect he desires. Millions of aspiring guitarists must have played the opening chords of 'Blowin' In The Wind' and wondered why it sounded different to Dylan's record – not realising that he had placed his capo on the 7th fret to produce that distinctively razor-sharp sound.

From 1965 onwards, when Dylan was often accompanied by a band of anything up to a dozen musicians, the subtleties of his guitar work were less obvious. Sometimes the most emblematic guitar figures on a song, such as 'Fourth Time Around' or 'Just Like A Woman', were delivered with or by a fellow musician in the studio. Sometimes, indeed, as on the studio rendition of 'Blind Willie McTell', Dylan eschewed the guitar entirely, allowing someone like Mark Knopfler to add his own decorations to Dylan's piano accompaniment.

On his early acoustic recordings, however, and again on his remarkable early 1990s ventures into the folk and blues heritage, the sheer dexterity of Dylan's guitar work is revealed. Take, for example, 'Masters Of War': not just a lyric and performance of blinding intensity, but an encapsulation of Dylan's guitar techniques, with picking, strumming and hammering combined almost unconsciously into a *tour de force* of musical expression. There's similar genius on display throughout this volume, which confirms that Bob Dylan's work as a guitarist is as deserving of our study and admiration as any aspect of his ever-changing art.

# Guitar Tablature Explained

## Guitar music can be notated in three different ways; on a musical stave, in tablature, and in rhythm slashes

**RHYTHM SLASHES:** are written above the stave. Strum chords in the rhythm indicated. Round noteheads indicate single notes.

**THE MUSICAL STAVE:** shows pitches and rhythms and is divided by lines into bars. Pitches are named after the first seven letters of the alphabet.

**TABLATURE:** graphically represents the guitar fingerboard. Each horizontal line represents a string, and each number represents a fret.

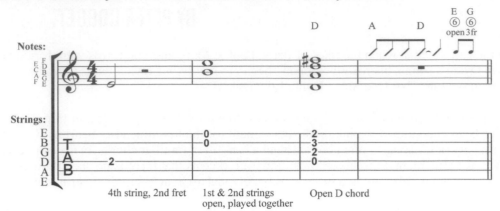

4th string, 2nd fret    1st & 2nd strings open, played together    Open D chord

## Definitions for special guitar notation

**SEMI-TONE BEND:** Strike the note and bend up a semi-tone (½ step).

**WHOLE-TONE BEND:** Strike the note and bend up a whole-tone (full step).

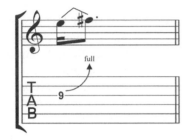

**GRACE NOTE BEND:** Strike the note and bend as indicated. Play the first note as quickly as possible.

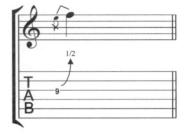

**QUARTER-TONE BEND:** Strike the note and bend up a ¼ step

**BEND & RELEASE:** Strike the note and bend up as indicated, then release back to the original note.

**COMPOUND BEND & RELEASE:** Strike the note and bend up and down in the rhythm indicated.

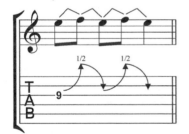

**PRE-BEND:** Bend the note as indicated, then strike it.

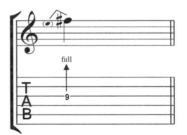

**PRE-BEND & RELEASE:** Bend the note as indicated. Strike it and release the note back to the original pitch.

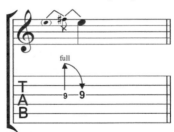

**HAMMER-ON:** Strike the first note with one finger, then sound the second note (on the same string) with another finger by fretting it without picking.

**PULL-OFF:** Place both fingers on the note to be sounded, strike the first note and without picking, pull the finger off to sound the second note.

**LEGATO SLIDE (GLISS):** Strike the first note and then slide the same fret-hand finger up or down to the second note. The second note is not struck.

**MUFFLED STRINGS:** A percussive sound is produced by laying the first hand across the string(s) without depressing, and striking them with the pick hand.

**NATURAL HARMONIC:** Strike the note while the fret-hand lightly touches the string directly over the fret indicated.

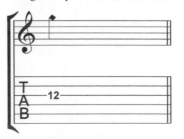

**PICK SCRAPE:** The edge of the pick is rubbed down (or up) the string, producing a scratchy sound.

**PALM MUTING:** The note is partially muted by the pick hand lightly touching the string(s) just before the bridge.

**SHIFT SLIDE (GLISS & RESTRIKE)** Same as legato slide, except the second note is struck.

**TAP HARMONIC:** The note is fretted normally and a harmonic is produced by tapping or slapping the fret indicated in brackets (which will be twelve frets higher than the fretted note.)

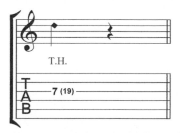

**TAPPING:** Hammer ('tap') the fret indicated with the pick-hand index or middle finger and pull-off to the note fretted by the fret hand.

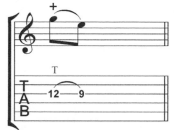

**PINCH HARMONIC:** The note is fretted normally and a harmonic is produced by adding the edge of the thumb or the tip of the index finger of the pick hand to the normal pick attack.

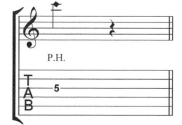

**ARTIFICIAL HARMONIC:** The note fretted normally and a harmonic is produced by gently resting the pick hand's index finger directly above the indicated fret (in brackets) while plucking the appropriate string.

**TRILL:** Very rapidly alternate between the notes indicated by continuously hammering-on and pulling-off.

**RAKE:** Drag the pick across the strings with a single motion.

**TREMOLO PICKING:** The note is picked as rapidly and continously as possible.

**ARPEGGIATE:** Play the notes of the chord indicated by quickly rolling them from bottom to top.

**SWEEP PICKING:** Rhythmic downstroke and/or upstroke motion across the strings.

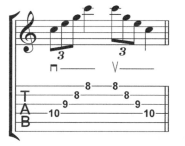

**VIBRATO DIVE BAR AND RETURN:** The pitch of the note or chord is dropped a specific number of steps (in rhythm) then returned to the original pitch.

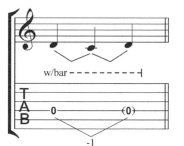

**VIBRATO BAR SCOOP:** Depress the bar just before striking the note, then quickly release the bar.

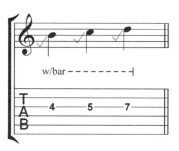

**VIBRATO BAR DIP:** Strike the note and then immediately drop a specific number of steps, then release back to the original pitch.

# Additional musical definitions

| | | |
|---|---|---|
| (accent) | Accentuate note (play it louder) | **D.S. al Coda** — Go back to the sign (𝄋), then play until the bar marked **To Coda** ⊕ then skip to the section marked ⊕ **Coda** |
| (accent) | Accentuate note with greater intensity | **D.C. al Fine** — Go back to the beginning of the song and play until the bar marked **Fine.** |
| (staccato) | Shorten time value of note | tacet — Instrument is silent (drops out). |
| ⊓ | Downstroke | |
| V | Upstroke | Repeat bars between signs |

NOTE: Tablature numbers in brackets mean:
1. The note is sustained, but a new articulation (such as hammer-on or slide) begins
2. A note may be fretted but not necessarily played.

When a repeat section has different endings, play the first ending only the first time and the second ending only the second time.

# BALLAD OF HOLLIS BROWN

**Words & Music by Bob Dylan**

†Symbols in parentheses represent names with respect to capoed guitar. Symbols above represent actual sounding chords.
Tab numbering represents non-capoed guitar (Tab 0 = 1 fr.).

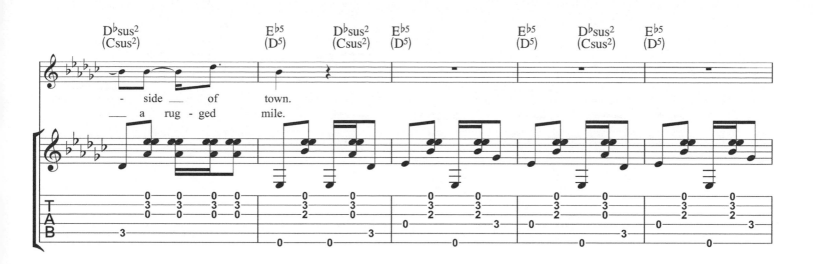

— side ___ of town.
___ a rug-ged mile.

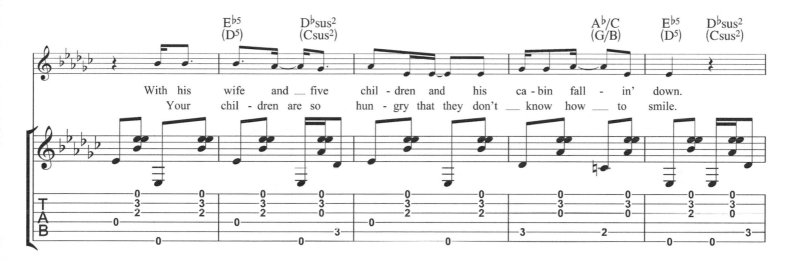

With his wife and ___ five chil-dren and his ca-bin fall-in' down.
Your chil-dren are so hun-gry that they don't ___ know how ___ to smile.

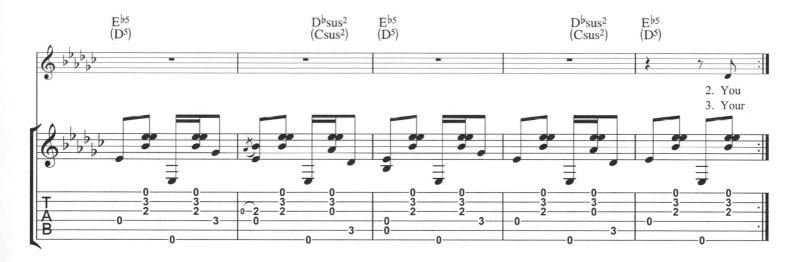

2. You
3. Your

ba-by's eyes ___ look cra-zy they're a-tug-gin' at ___ your sleeve,

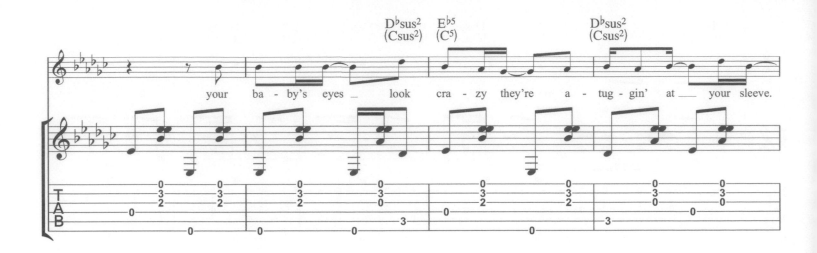

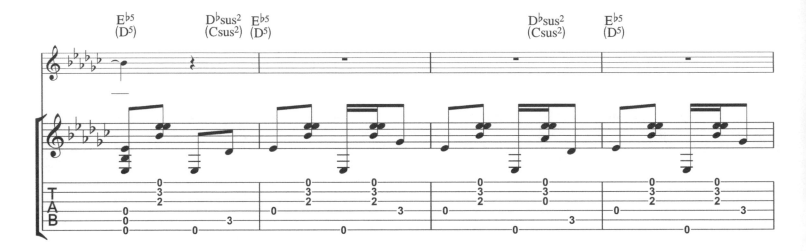

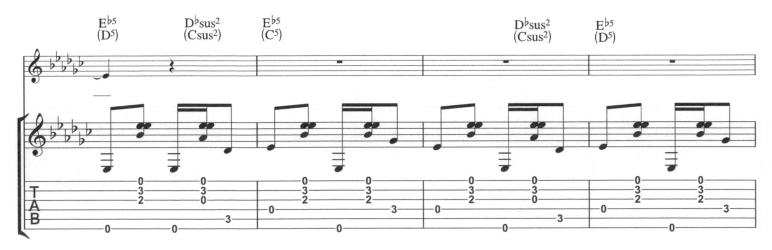

8

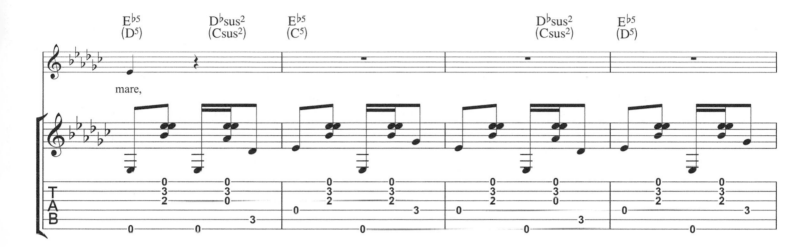

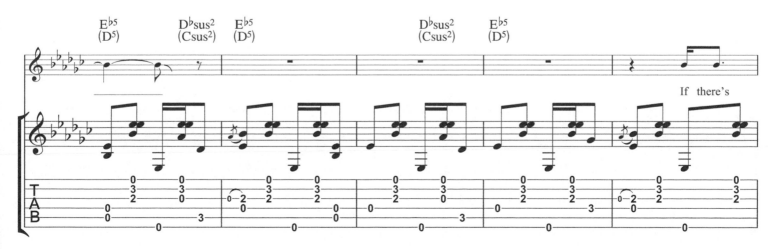

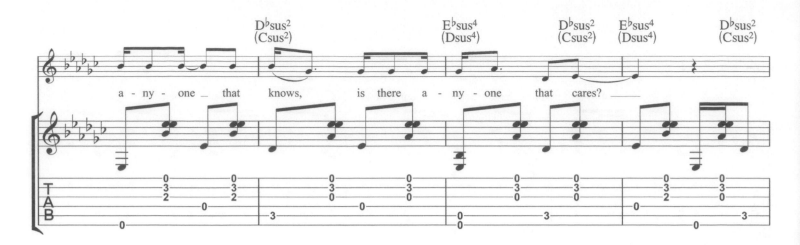

a - ny - one ___ that knows, is there a - ny - one that cares? ___

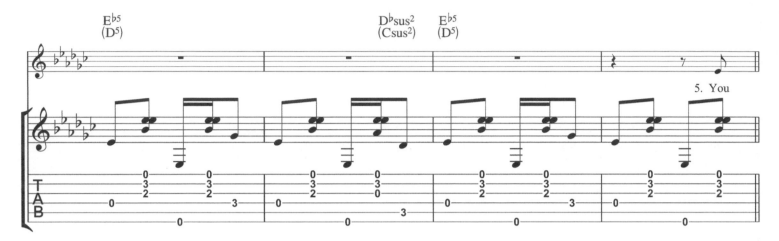

5. You

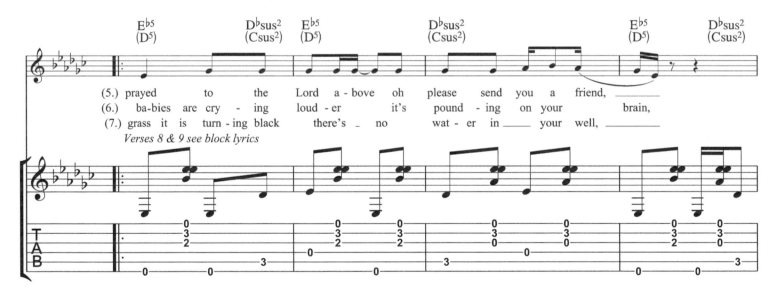

(5.) prayed to the Lord a - bove oh please send you a friend, ___
(6.) ba-bies are cry - ing loud - er it's pound - ing on your brain,
(7.) grass it is turn - ing black there's _ no wat - er in ___ your well, ___
*Verses 8 & 9 see block lyrics*

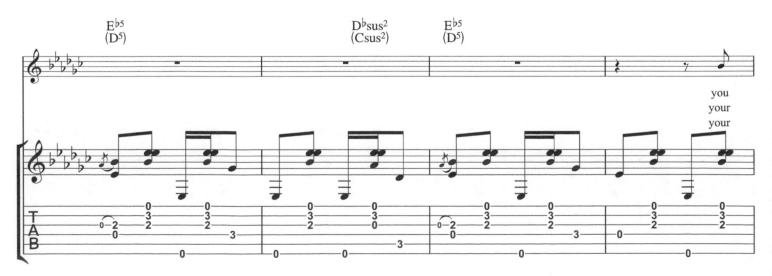

you
your
your

10

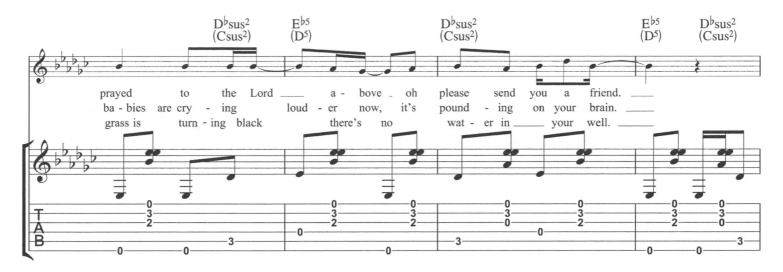

prayed    to    the Lord ____ a - bove ___ oh    please    send    you    a    friend. ____
ba - bies    are cry - ing    loud - er    now, it's    pound - ing    on    your    brain. ____
grass is    turn - ing    black    there's    no    wat - er in ____ your    well. ____

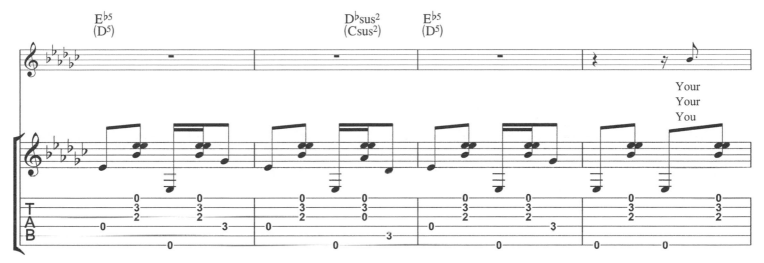

Your
Your
You

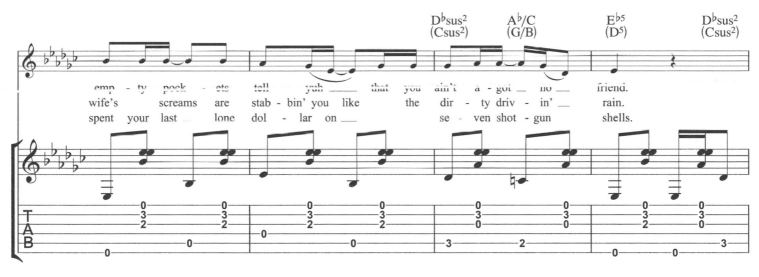

emp - ty    pock - ets    tell    yuh ____ that    you    ain't    a - got ___ no ___ friend.
wife's    screams    are    stab - bin' you    like    the    dir - ty driv - in' ___ rain.
spent    your    last    lone    dol - lar    on ___ se - ven    shot - gun    shells.

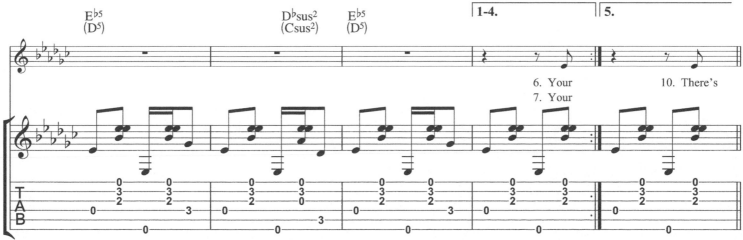

6. Your          10. There's
7. Your

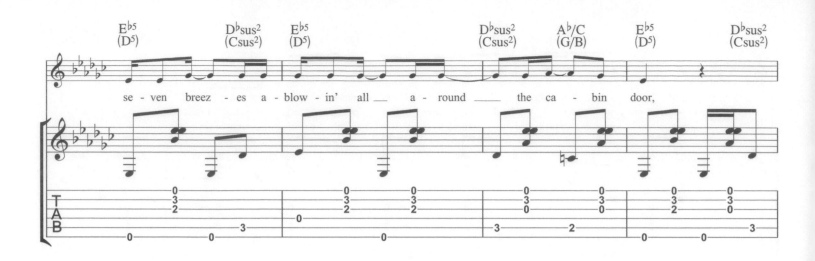

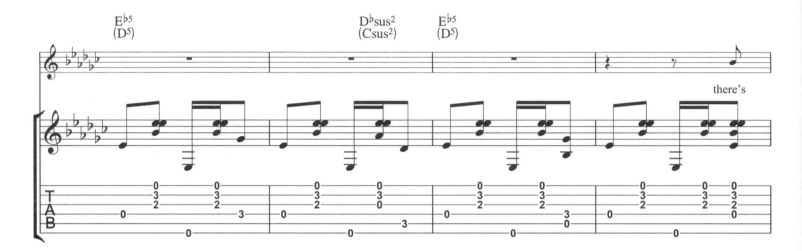

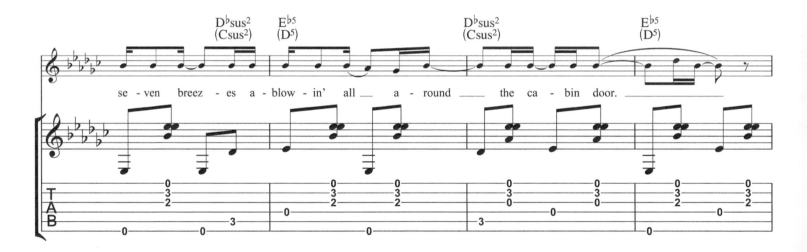

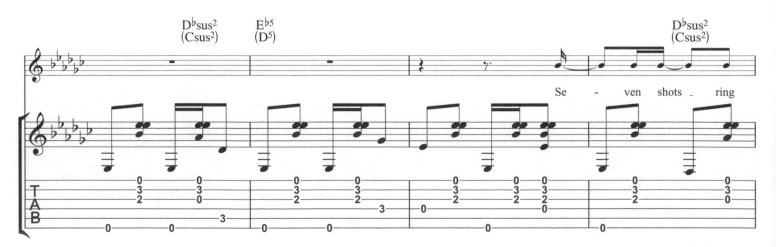

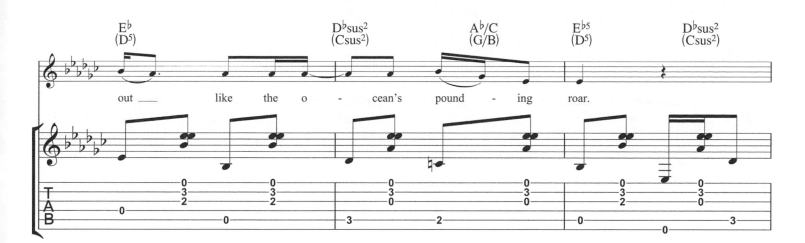

out ___ like the o - cean's pound - ing roar.

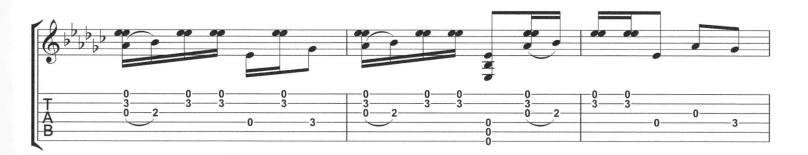

**Instrumental**

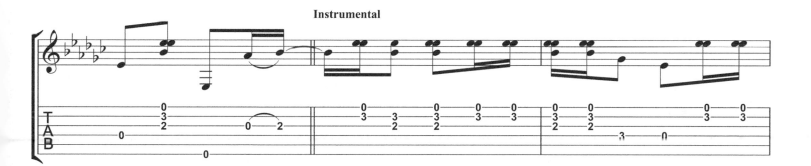

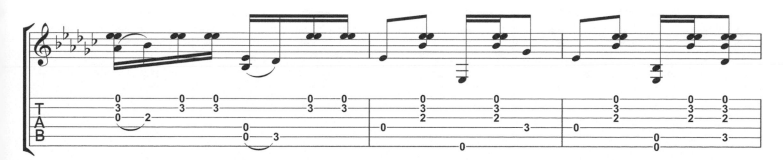

13

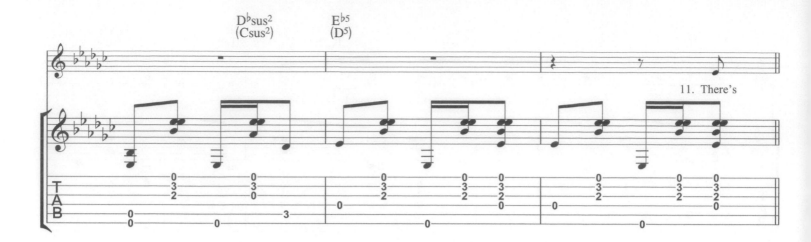

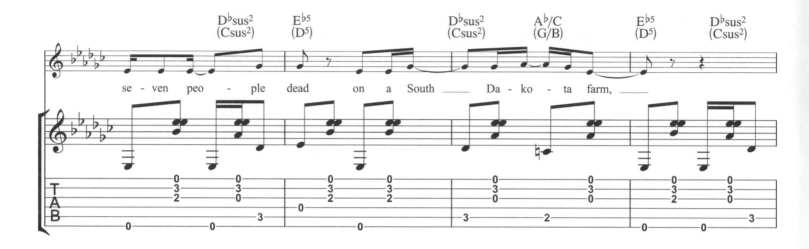

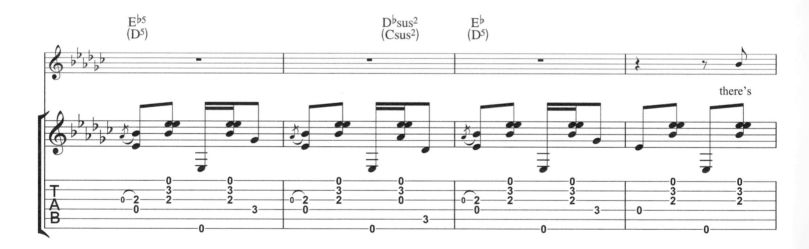

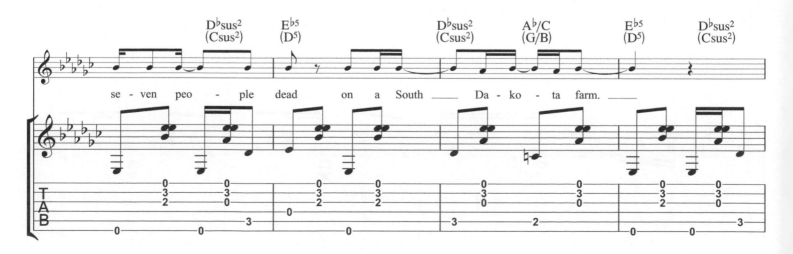

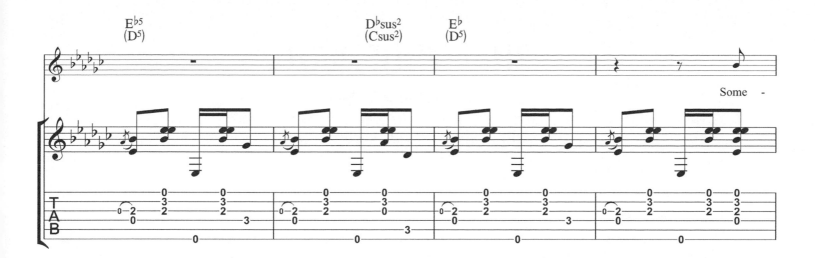

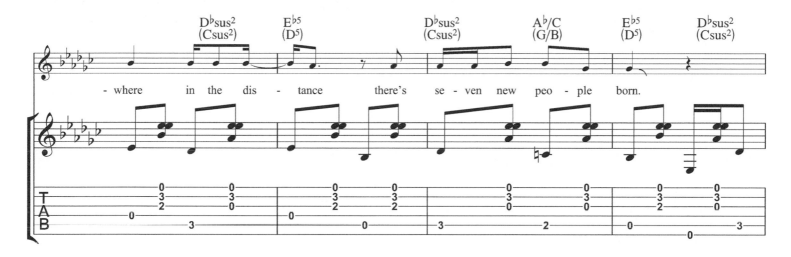

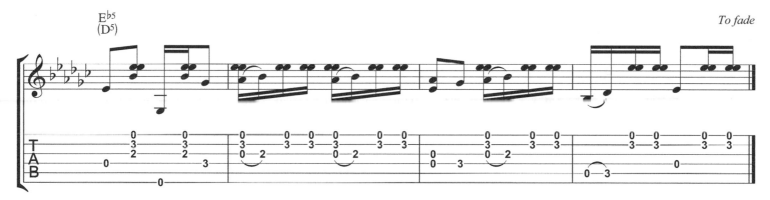

*Verse 8:*
Way out in the wilderness
A cold coyote calls
Way out in the wilderness
A cold coyote calls
Your eyes fix on the shotgun
That's hangin' on the wall

*Verse 9:*
Your brain is a-bleedin'
And your legs can't seem to stand
Your brain is a-bleedin'
And your legs can't seem to stand
Your eyes fix on the shotgun
That you're holdin' in your hand

# BLIND WILLIE McTELL

### Words & Music by Bob Dylan

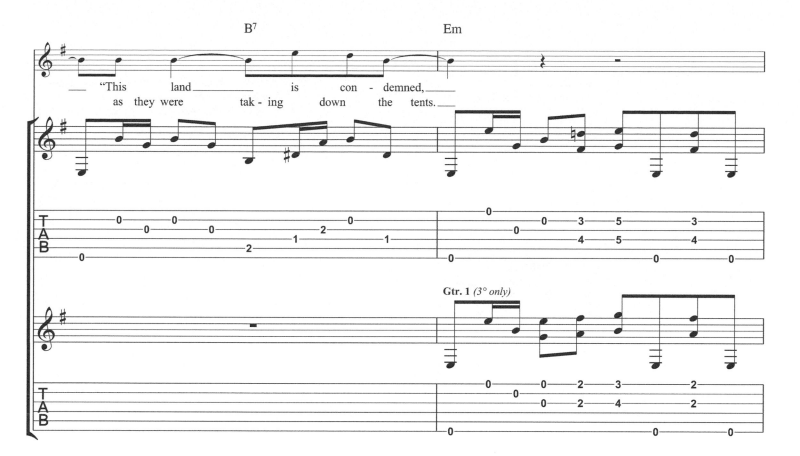

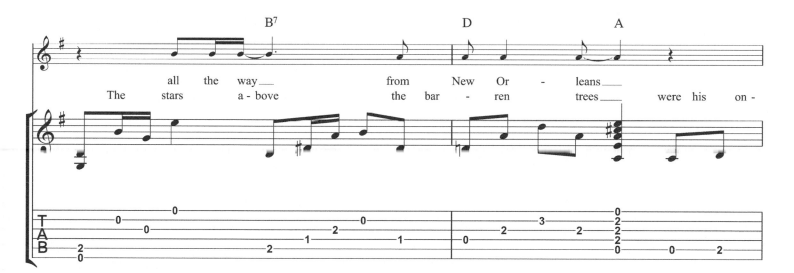

17

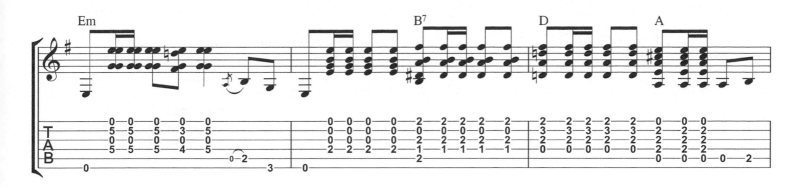

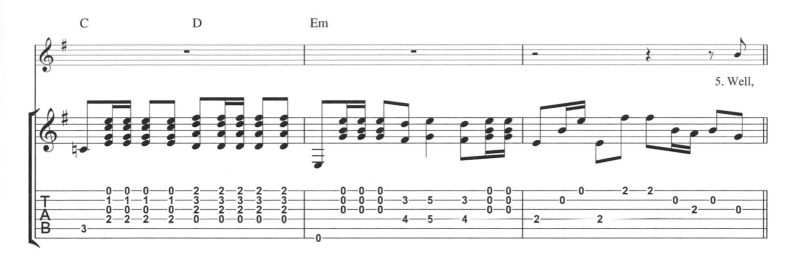

### Verse

Gtr. 1 plays Fig. 1

God is in_ His hea - ven_____ and we all_____ want what's His._

But pow-er and greed_ and cor-rupt-i - ble_ seed_ seem_____ to be all_ that there is._

_ I'm gaz - ing out_ the win - dow_____

of the St. James_ ho - tel._____ And I_ know no_ one_

can sing the blues_____ like Blind Wil - lie_____ Mc - Tell._____

Outro

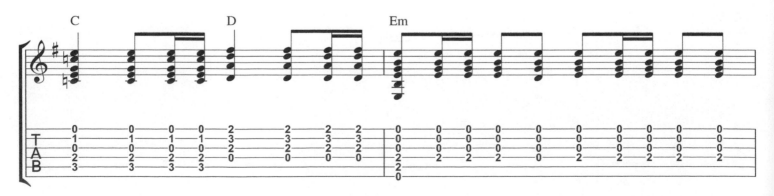

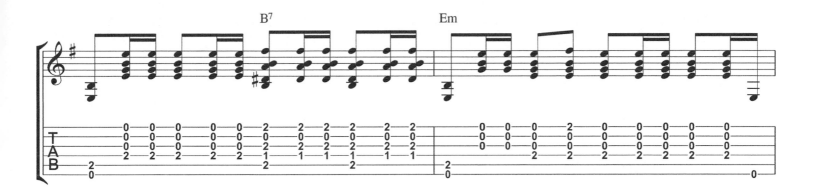

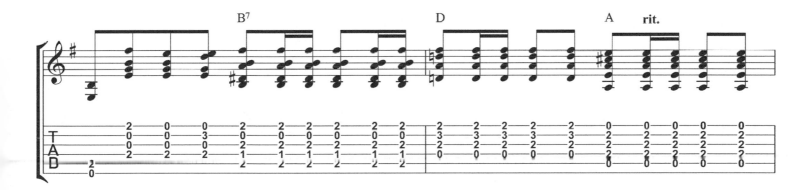

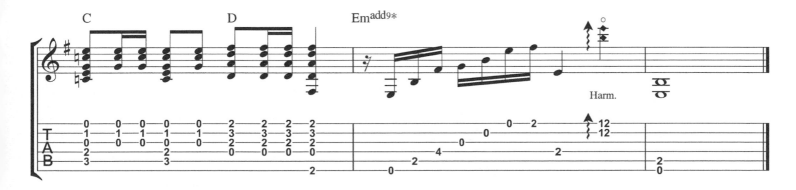

*Verse 3:*
See them big plantations burning
Hear the cracking of the whips
Smell that sweet magnolia blooming
See the ghosts of slavery ships
I can hear them tribes a-moaning
Hear the undertaker's bell
Nobody can sing the blues
Like Blind Willie McTell

*Verse 4:*
There's a woman by the river
With some fine young handsome man
He's dressed up like a squire
Bootlegged whiskey in his hand
There's a chain gang on the highway
I can hear them rebels yell
And I know no one can sing the blues
Like Blind Willie McTell

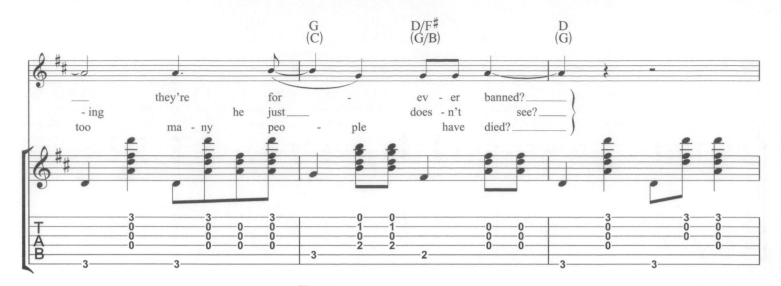

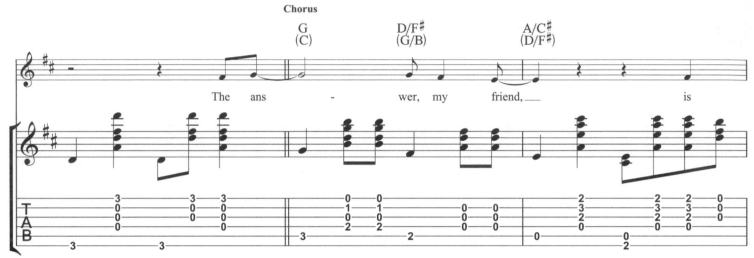

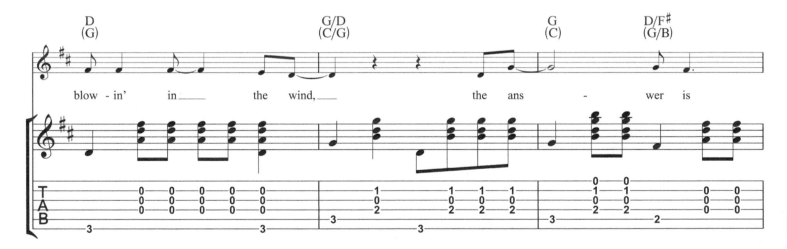

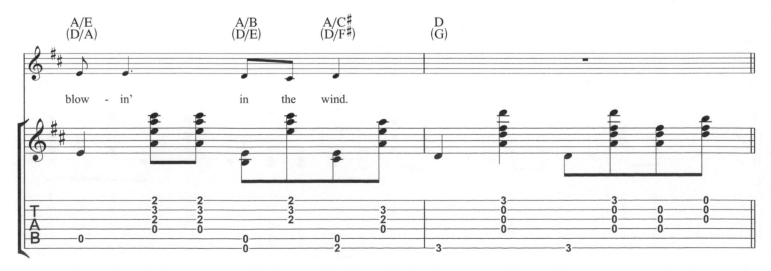

# BUCKETS OF RAIN

**Words & Music by Bob Dylan**

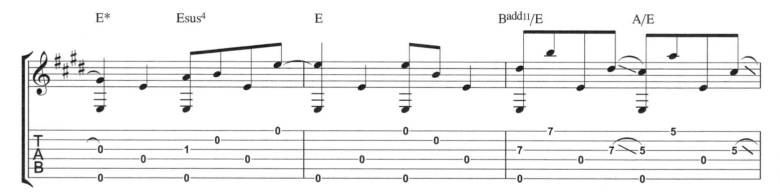

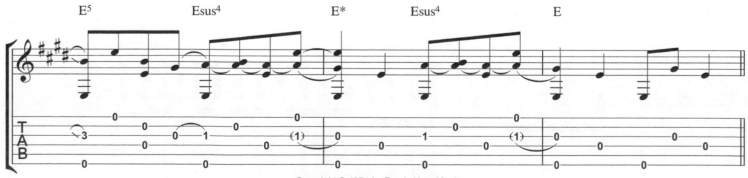

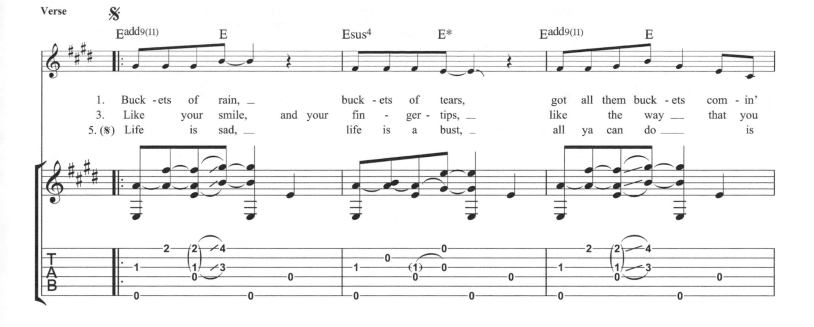

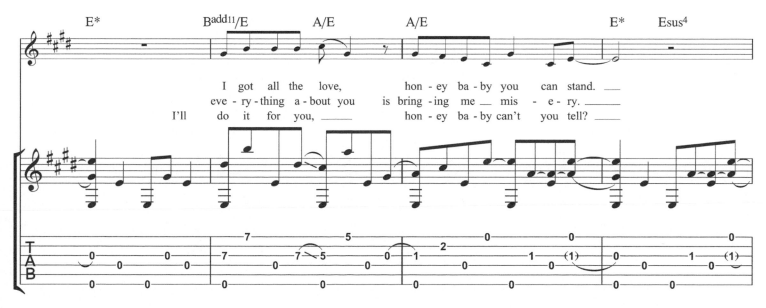

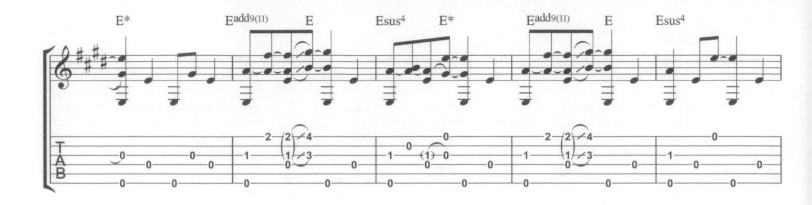

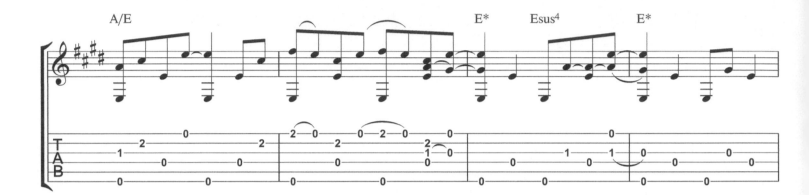

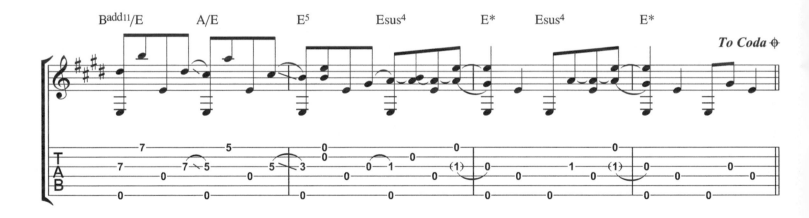

**Verse**

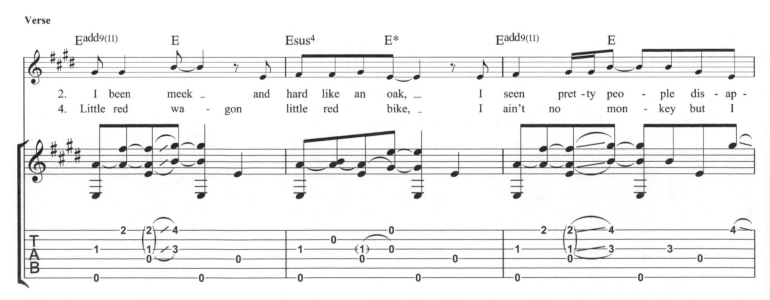

2. I been meek _ and hard like an oak, _ I seen pret-ty peo - ple dis - ap-
4. Little red wa - gon little red bike, _ I ain't no mon - key but I

28

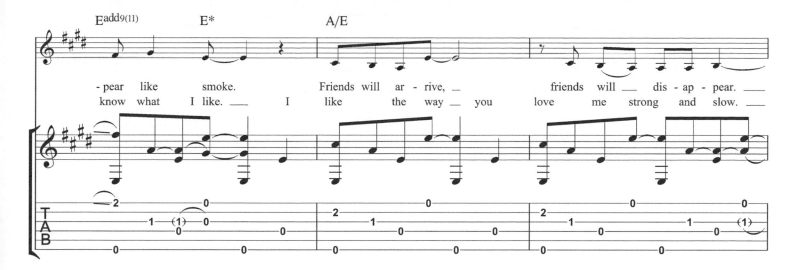

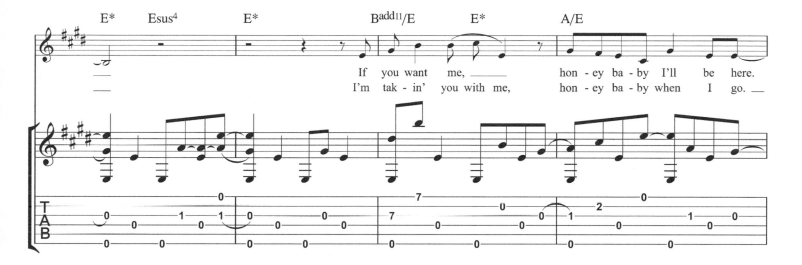

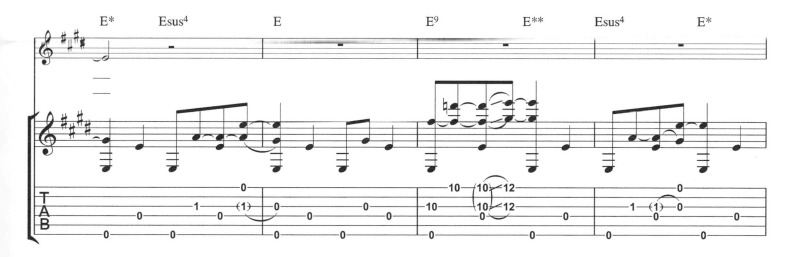

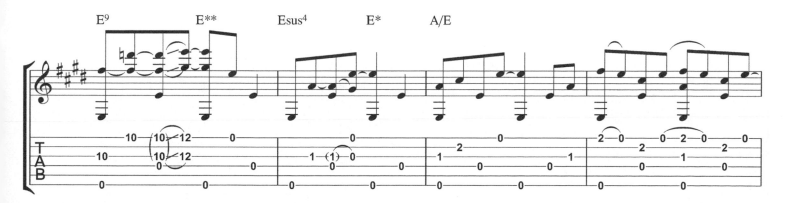

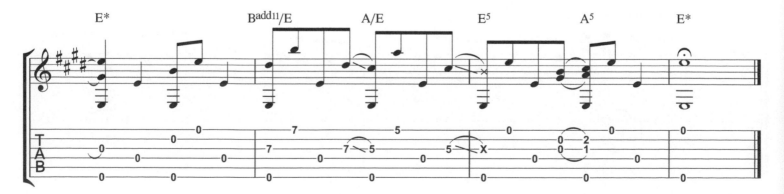

# I SHALL BE RELEASED

### Words & Music by Bob Dylan

**Capo 2nd fret**

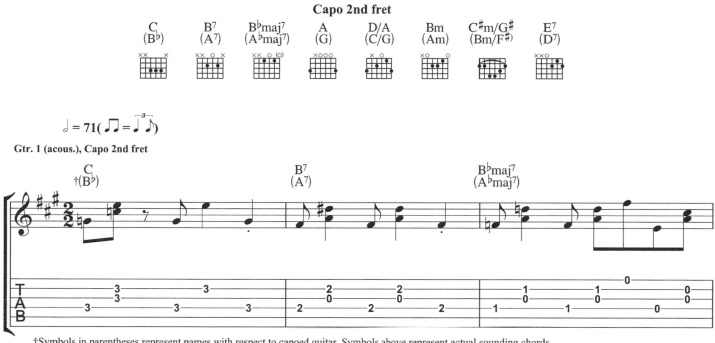

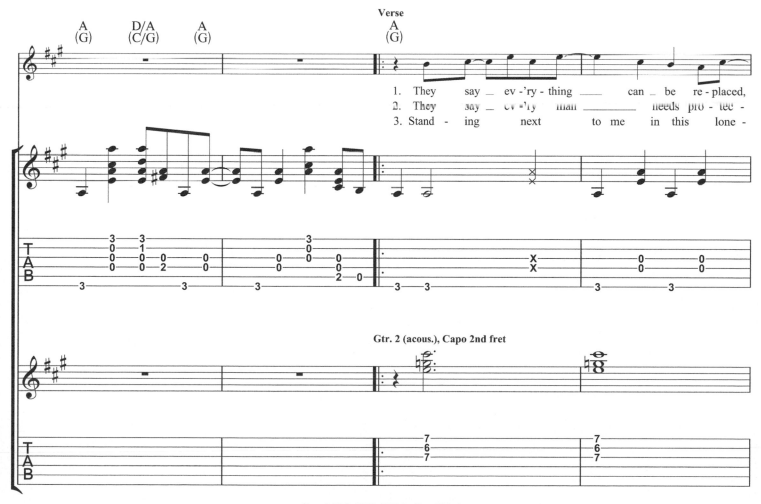

†Symbols in parentheses represent names with respect to capoed guitar. Symbols above represent actual sounding chords.
Tab numbering represents non-capoed guitar (Tab 0 = 2nd fret).

**Gtr. 2 (acous.), Capo 2nd fret**

1. They say ev-'ry-thing can be re-placed,
2. They say ev-'ry man needs pro-tec-
3. Stand-ing next to me in this lone-

face _____
-flec - tion, _____
so     loud, ___

of  ev - 'ry ____ man who put  me here. ___
some place  so ____ high  a-bove this wall. ___
cry - ing  out  that he was   framed, ___

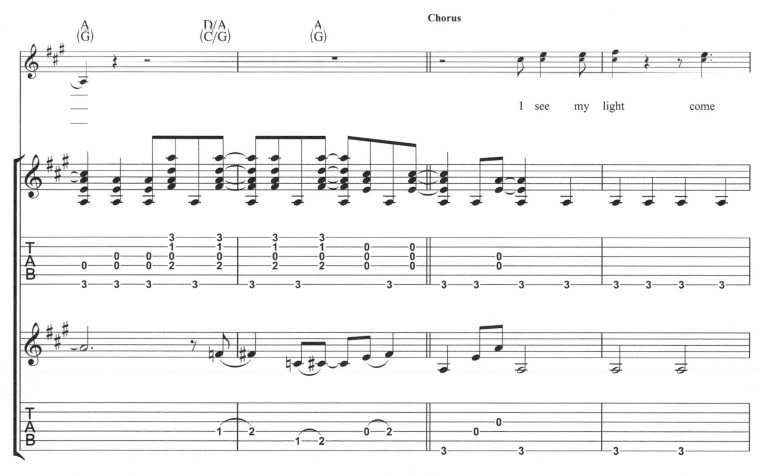

**Chorus**

I  see   my  light     come

34

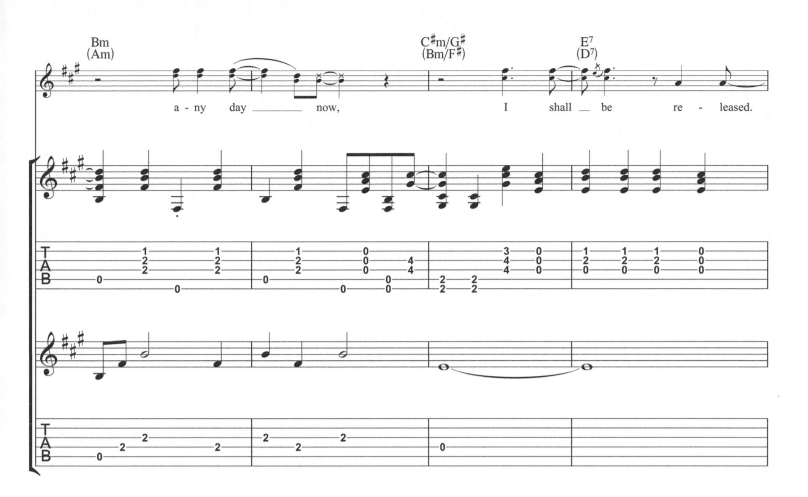

a - ny day _____ now,     I shall _ be    re - leased.

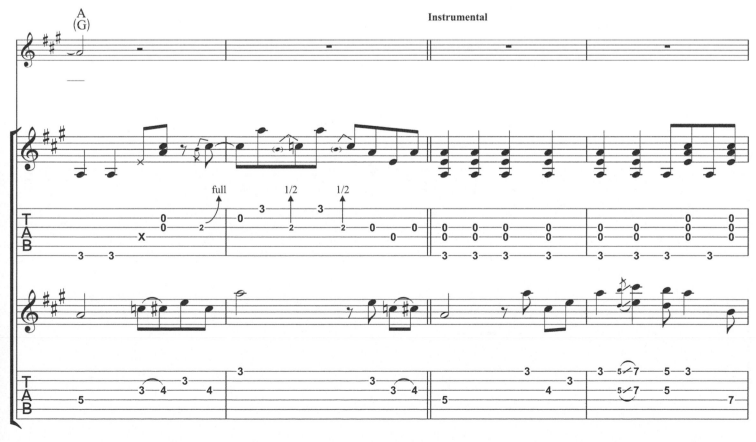

**Instrumental**

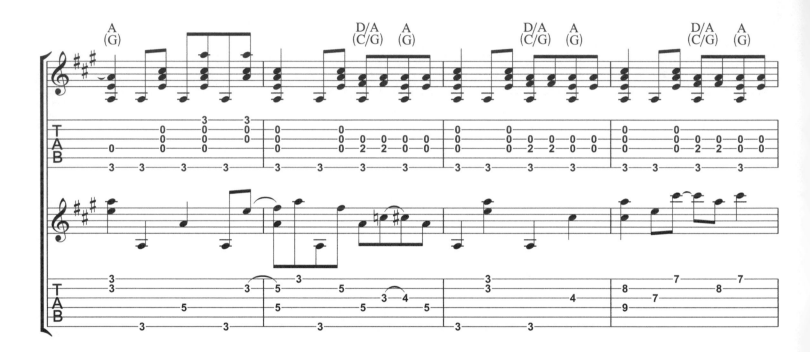

36

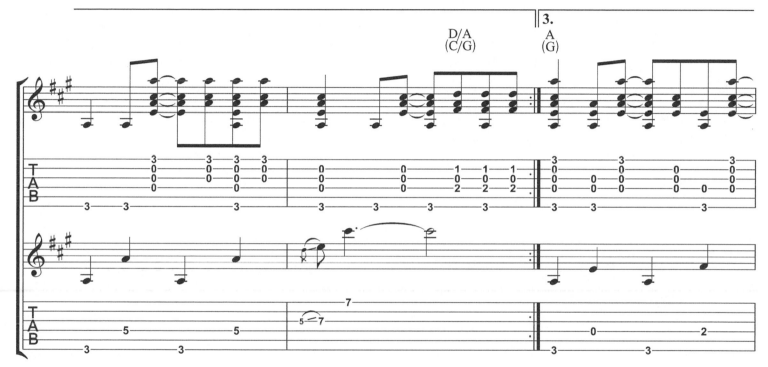

# DON'T THINK TWICE, IT'S ALL RIGHT

### Words & Music by Bob Dylan

†Symbols in parentheses represent names with respect to capoed guitar. Symbols above represent actual sounding chords.
Tab numbering represents non-capoed guitar (Tab 0 = 4 fr.).

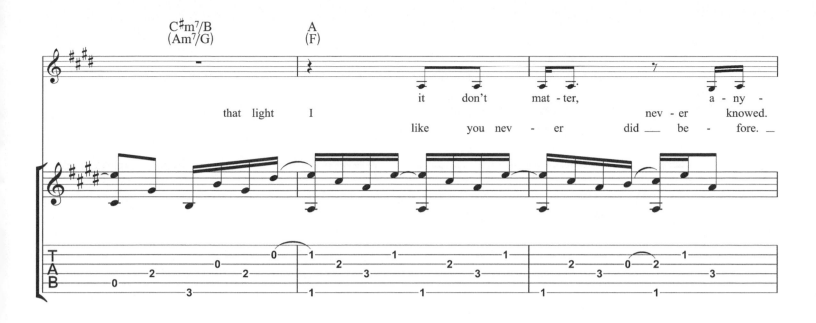

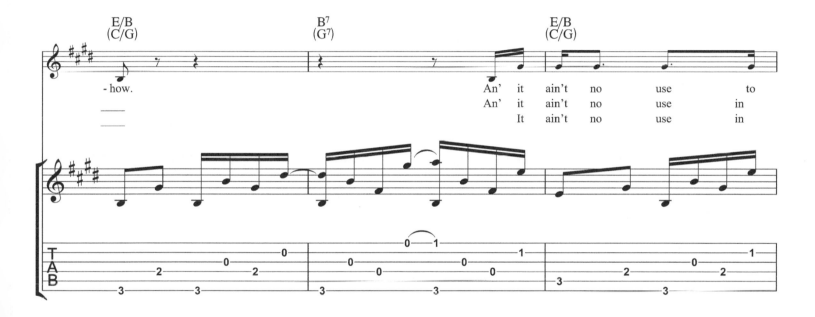

win - dow and _____ I'll be gone,
make me change my mind and stay.
wo - man, a child _____ I'm _____ told, I

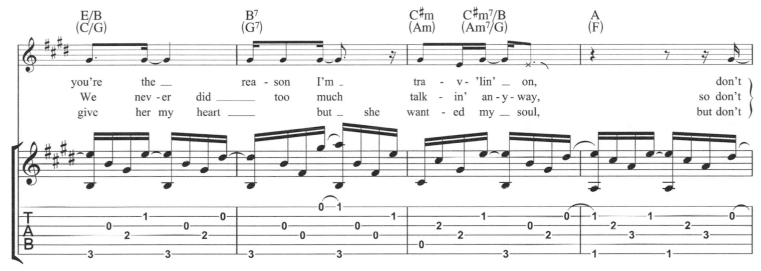

you're the __ rea - son I'm __ tra - v'lin' on, don't
We nev - er did _____ too much talk - in' an - y - way, so don't
give her my heart _____ but __ she want - ed my __ soul, but don't

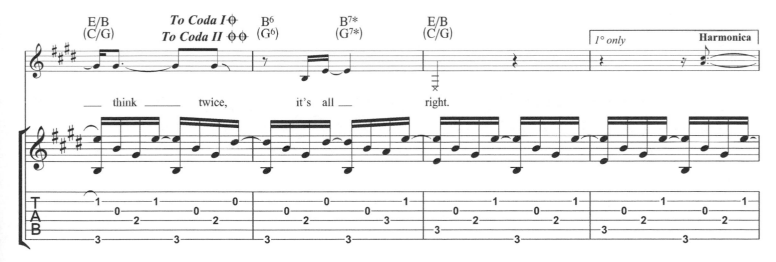

__ think _____ twice, it's all __ right.

*1° only*    **Harmonica**

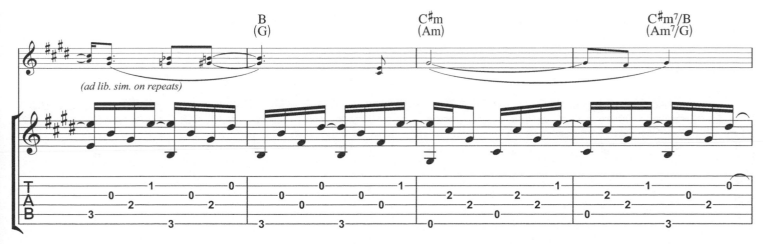

*(ad lib. sim. on repeats)*

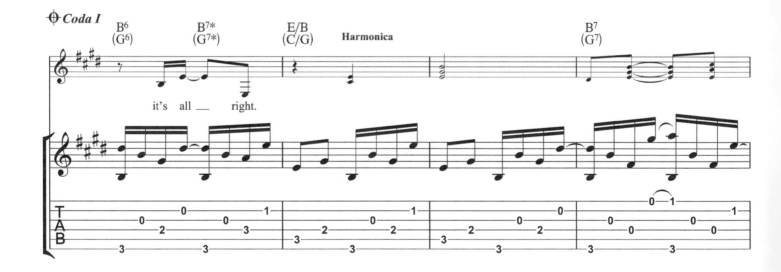

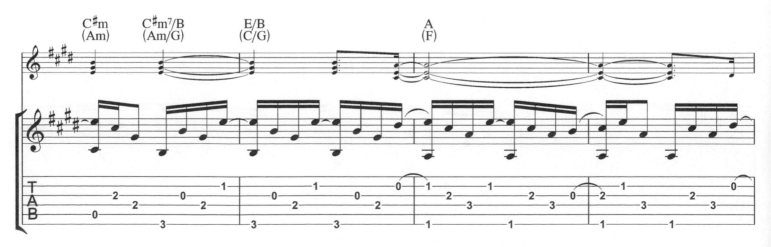

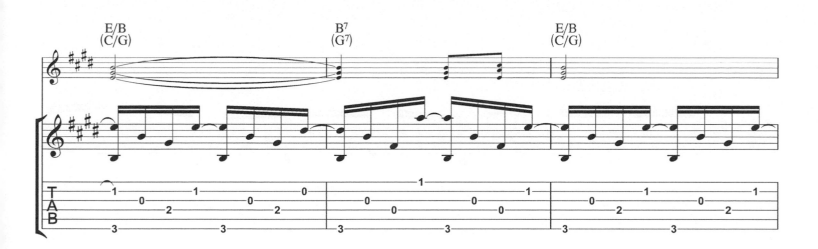

E/B
(C/G)

B⁷
(G⁷)

E/B
(C/G)

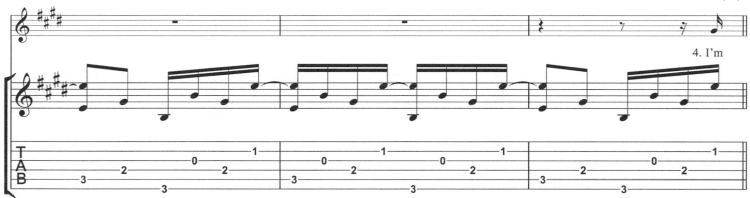

4. I'm

⊕ ⊕ *Coda II*

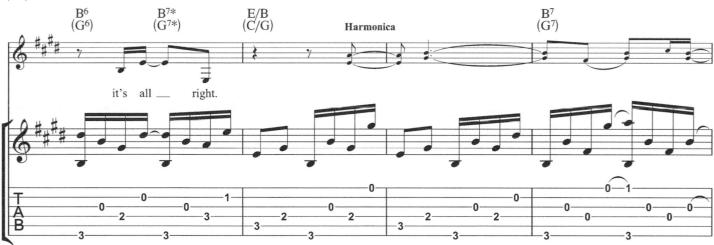

B⁶
(G⁶)

B⁷*
(G⁷*)

E/B
(C/G)

**Harmonica**

B⁷
(G⁷)

it's all __ right.

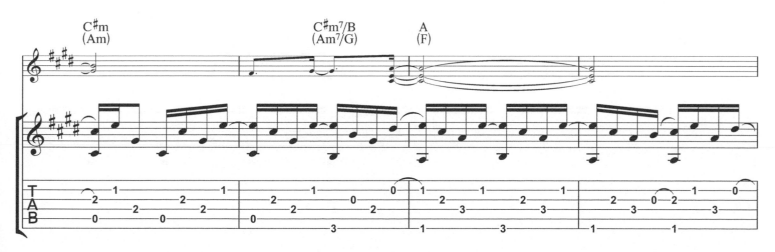

C♯m
(Am)

C♯m⁷/B
(Am⁷/G)

A
(F)

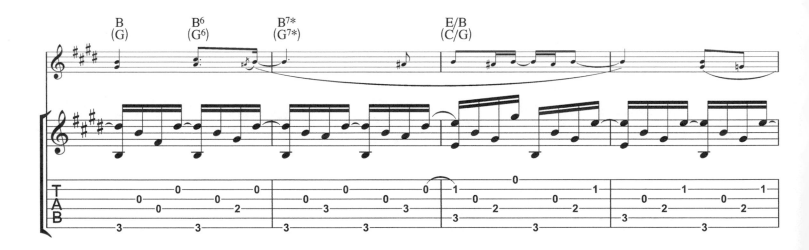

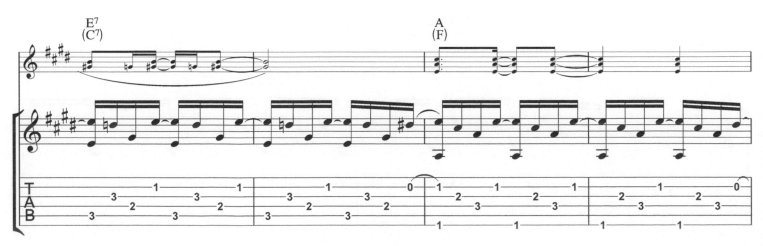

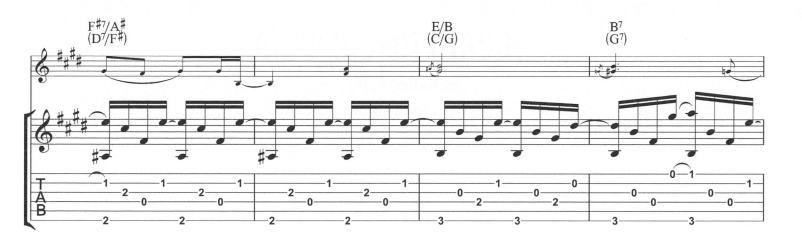

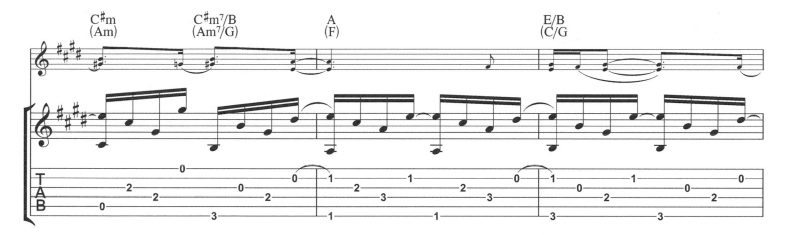

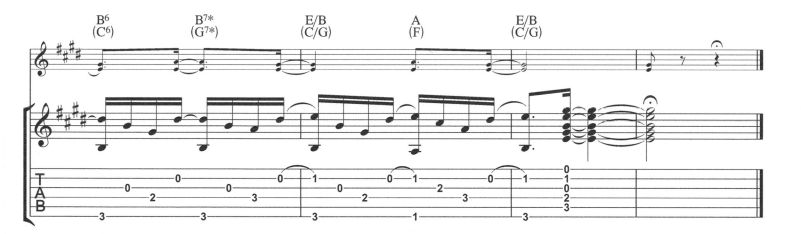

*Verse 4:*
I'm walkin' down that long, lonesome road, babe
Where I'm bound, I can't tell
But goodbye's too good a word, gal
So I'll just say fare thee well
I ain't sayin' you treated me unkind
You could have done better but I don't mind
You just kinda wasted my precious time
But don't think twice, it's all right

# FOURTH TIME AROUND

**Words & Music by Bob Dylan**

†Symbols in parentheses represent chord names with respect to capoed guitar.
Symbols above represent actual sounding chords.

F#m
(Dm)

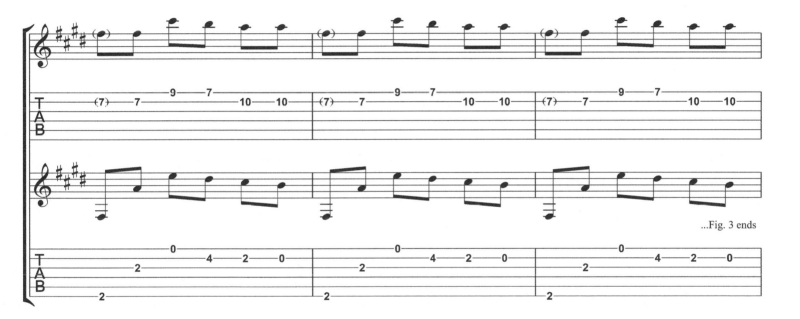

...Fig. 3 ends

E
(C)

Esus⁴
(Csus⁴)

E
(C)

Esus⁴
(Csus⁴)

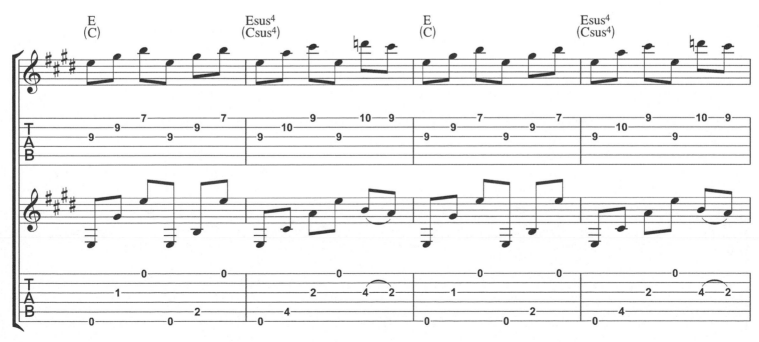

47

1. When

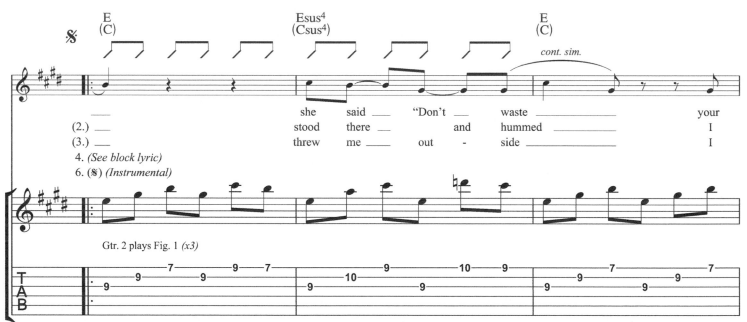

(2.) ___  she said ___ "Don't ___ waste _____ your
(3.) ___  stood there ___ and hummed _____ I
 4. *(See block lyric)*  threw me ___ out - side _____ I
 6. (𝄌) *(Instrumental)*

Gtr. 2 plays Fig. 1 *(x3)*

words, they're just ____ lies."          I cried ____ she was
tapped on her ____ drum _____          and asked her how come. ___
stood in the ____ dirt _____          where ev - 'ry - one walked. ___

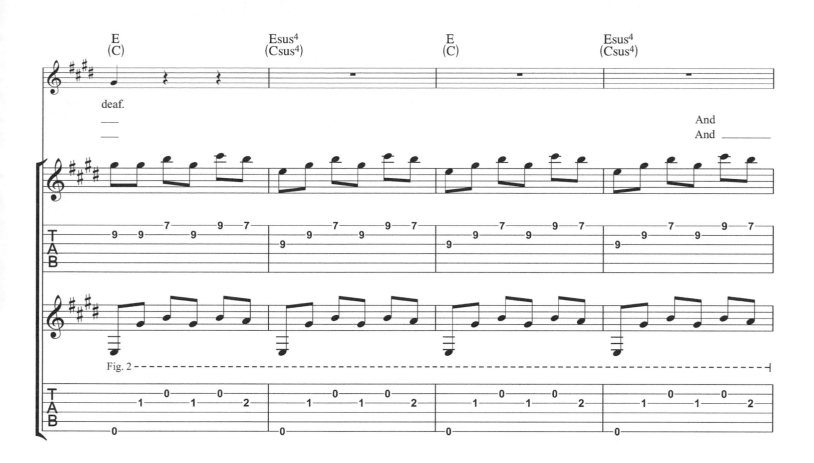

deaf.
___
___ And
And _____

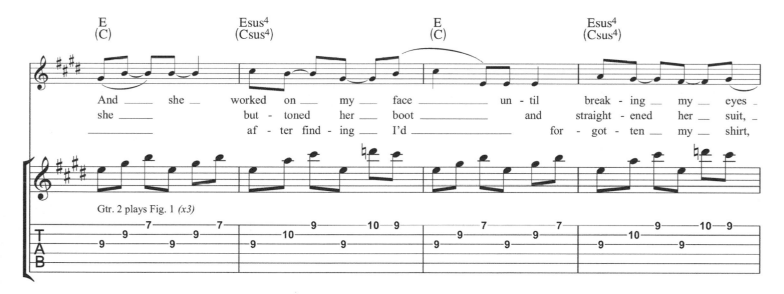

And _____ she _ worked on ___ my __ face _____ un - til break - ing __ my __ eyes __
she _____ but - toned her __ boot _____ and straight - ened her __ suit,
_____ af - ter find - ing __ I'd _____ for - got - ten __ my __ shirt,

Gtr. 2 plays Fig. 1 *(x3)*

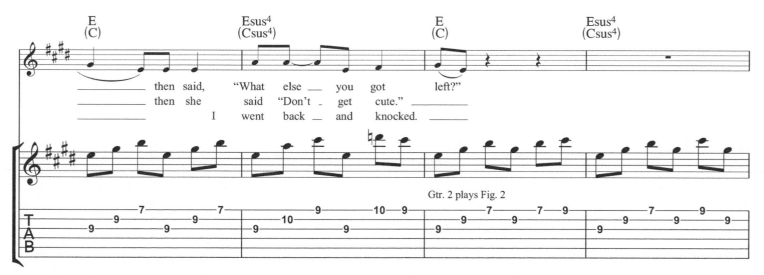

_____ then said, "What else __ you got ___ left?"
_____ then she said "Don't _ get cute."
_____ I went back __ and knocked.

Gtr. 2 plays Fig. 2

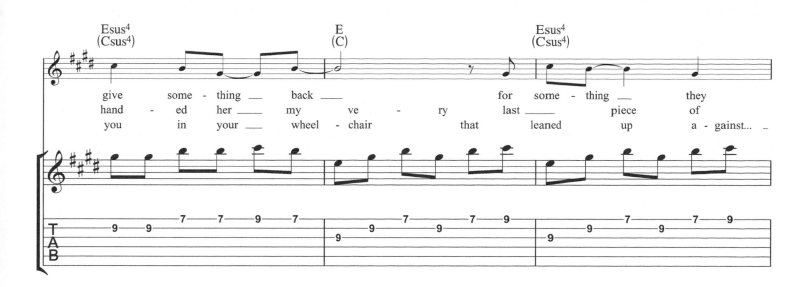

give some - thing ___ back ___ for some - thing ___ they
hand - ed her ___ my ve - ry last ____ piece of
you in your ___ wheel - chair that leaned up a - gainst... _

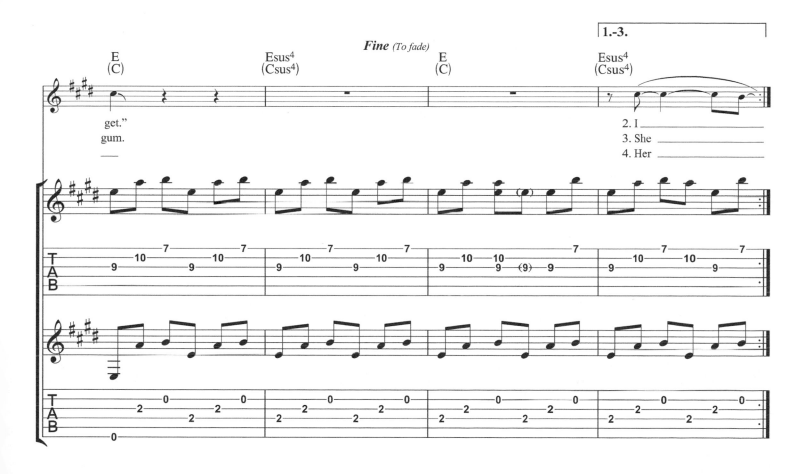

**Fine** *(To fade)*

**1.-3.**

get."
gum.
___

2. I _____
3. She _____
4. Her _____

**4.**

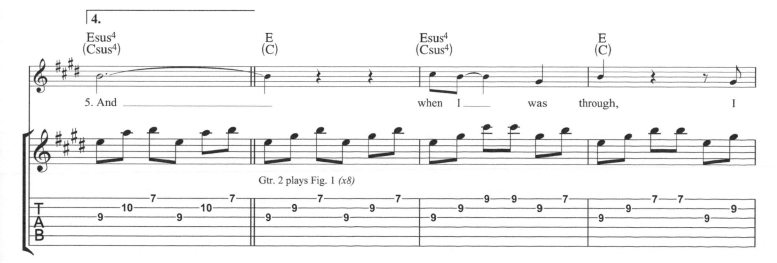

5. And _____ when I ___ was through, I

Gtr. 2 plays Fig. 1 *(x8)*

51

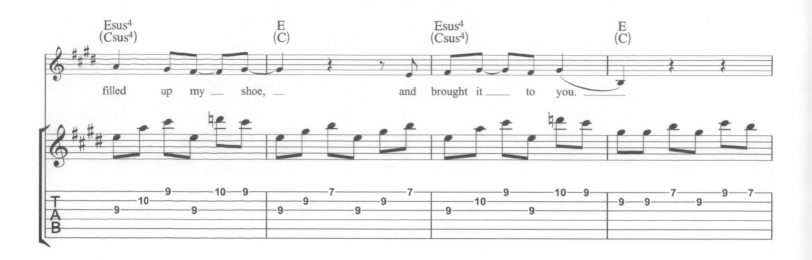

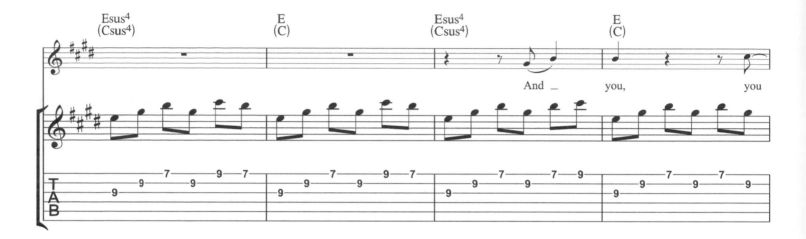

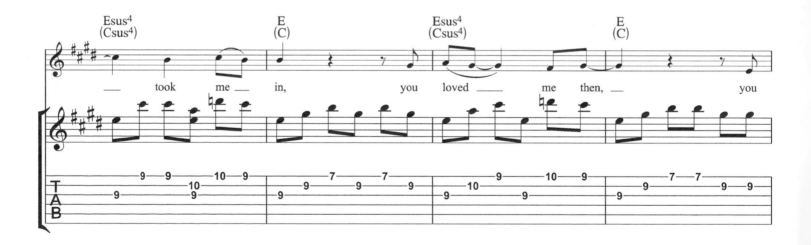

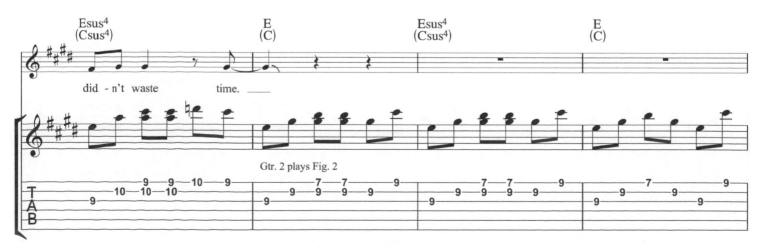

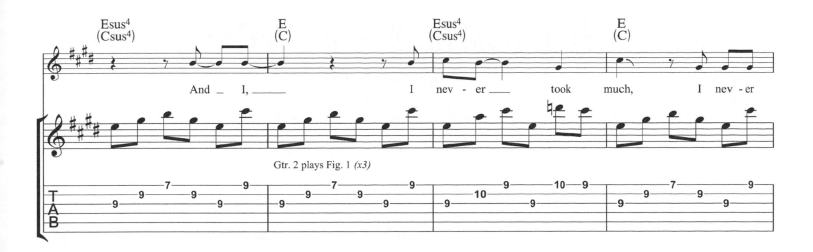

And __ I, _____ I nev - er ____ took much, I nev - er

Gtr. 2 plays Fig. 1 *(x3)*

asked for your ___ crutch, _ now don't ask ____ for mine. _

***D.S. al Fine***

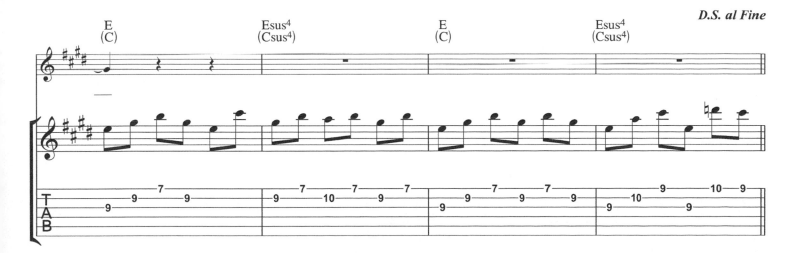

*Verse 4:*
Her Jamaican rum
And when she did come, I asked her for some
She said, "No, dear"
I said, "Your words aren't clear
You'd better spit out your gum"
She screamed till her face got so red
Then she fell on the floor
And I covered her up and then
Thought I'd go look through her drawer

# GIRL FROM THE NORTH COUNTRY

**Words & Music by Bob Dylan**

†Symbols in parentheses represent chord names with respect to capoed guitar. (Tab 0 = 3 fret.)
Symbols above represent actual sounding chords.

1. Well, if ___ you're
2. Well, if you go ___
5. So if ___ you're

tra-vel-in' ___ in the north ___ coun-try fair, ___
___ when the snow - flakes storm, ___
tra-vel-in' ___ in the north ___ coun-try fair, ___

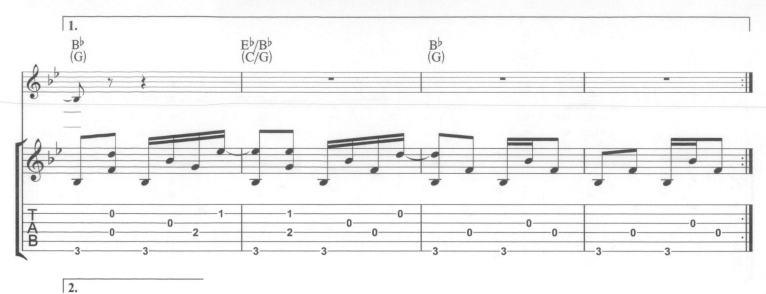

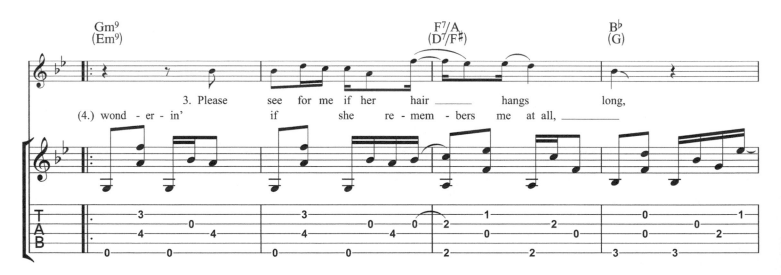

3. Please see for me if her hair _____ hangs long,

(4.) wond - er - in' if she re - mem - bers me at all, _____

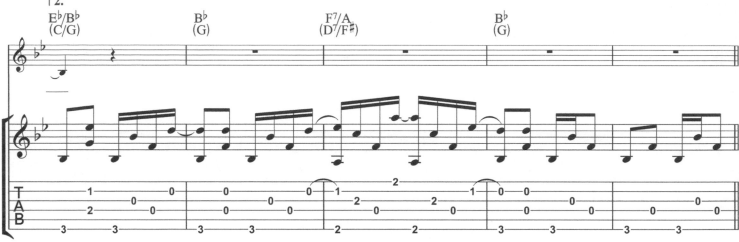

if it rolls _____ and flows all down her breast, __

ma - ny times I've of - ten prayed __

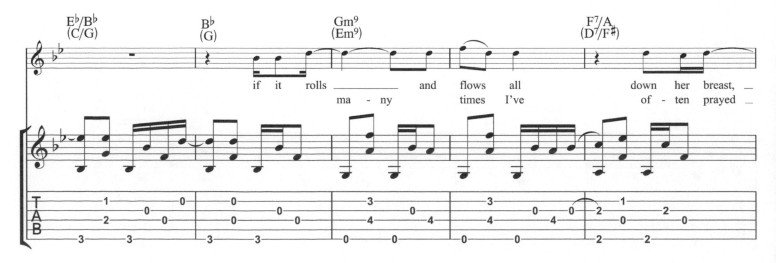

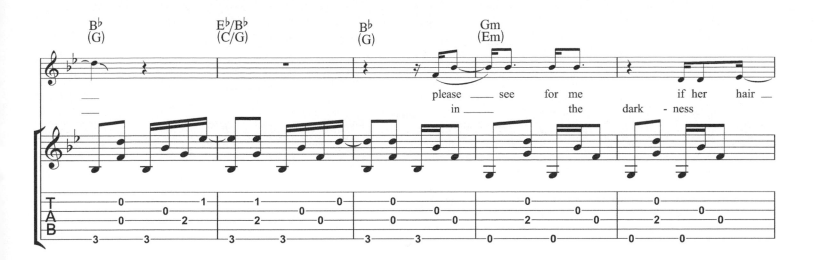

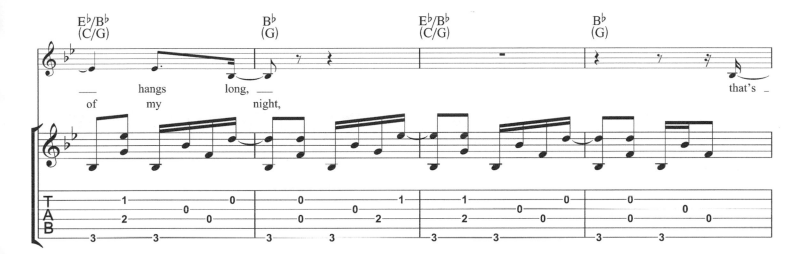

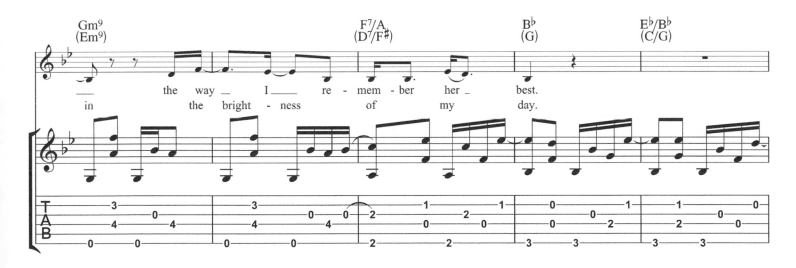

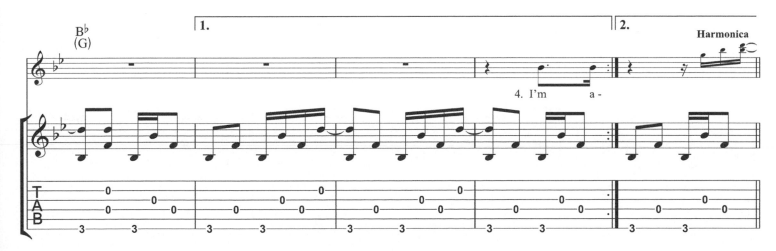

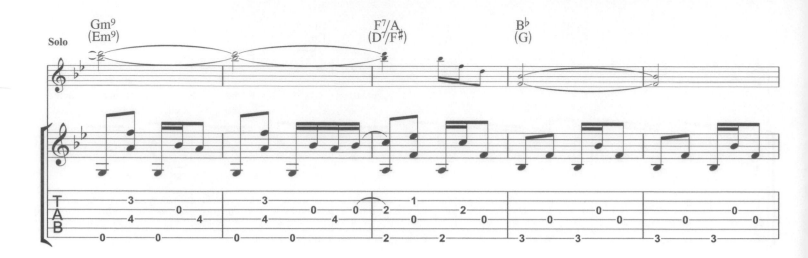

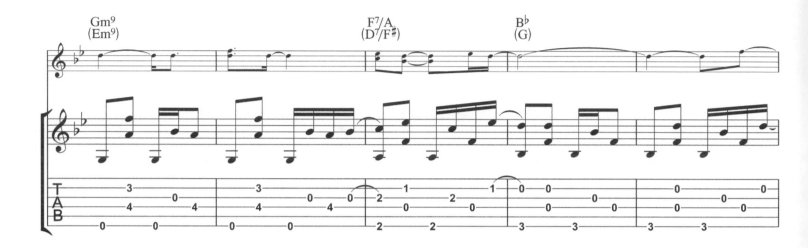

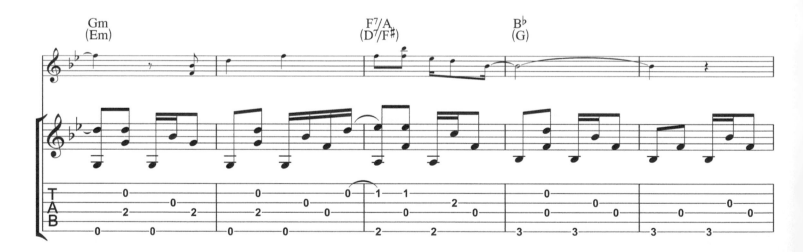

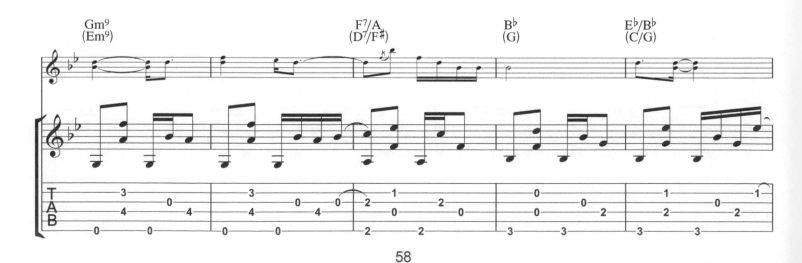

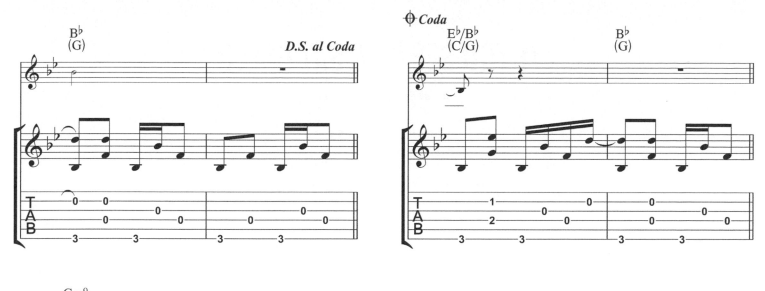

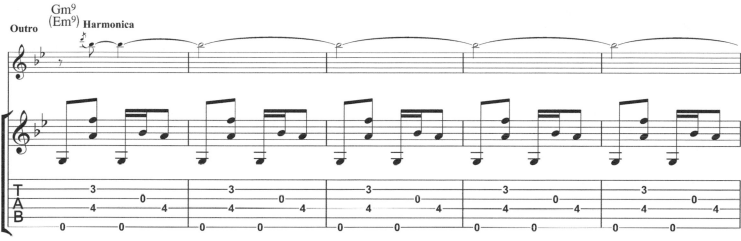

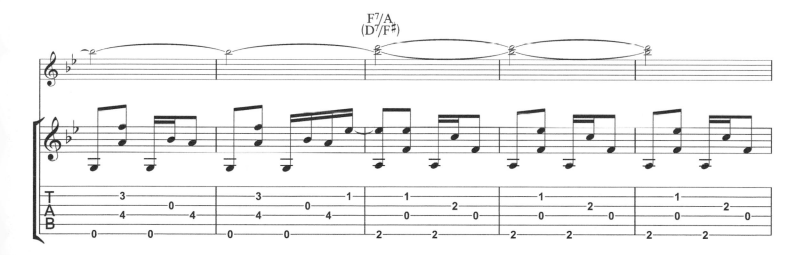

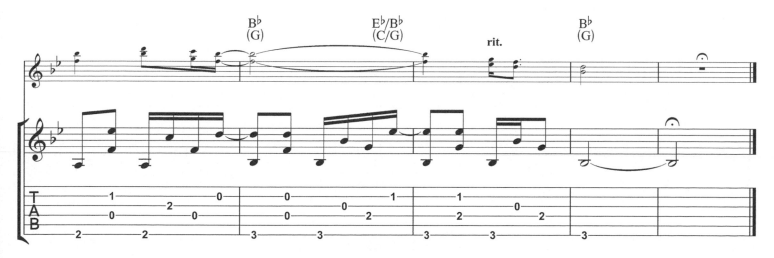

# IF YOU SEE HER, SAY HELLO

**Words & Music by Bob Dylan**

**Guitar 1: Capo 2nd fret**

†Symbols in parentheses represent chord names with respect to capoed guitar. (Tab 0 = 2 fr.)
Symbols above represent actual sounding chords.

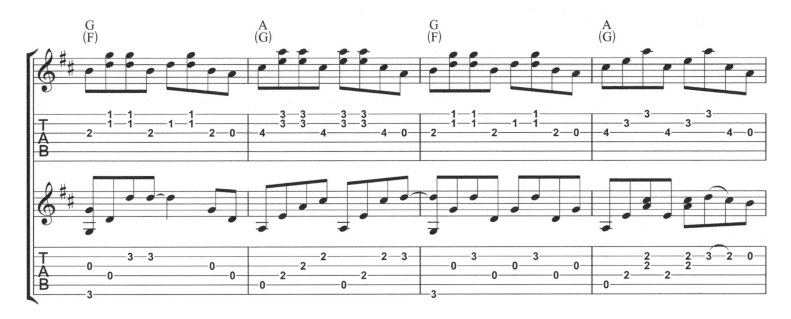

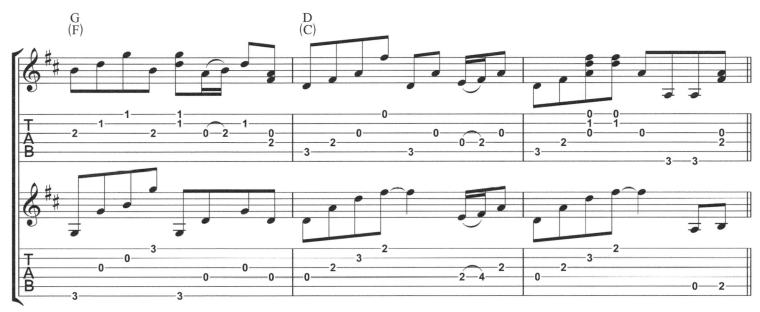

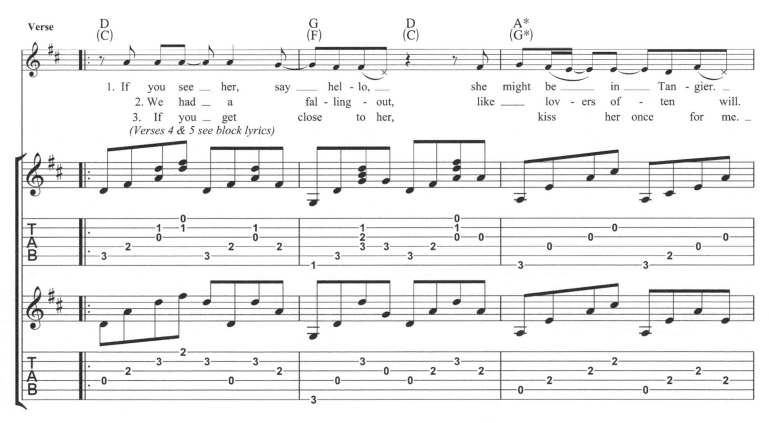

**Verse**

1. If you see __ her, say __ hel - lo, __ she might be _____ in __ Tan - gier. __
2. We had __ a fal - ling - out, like __ lov - ers of - ten will.
3. If you __ get close to her, kiss her once for me. __
*(Verses 4 & 5 see block lyrics)*

61

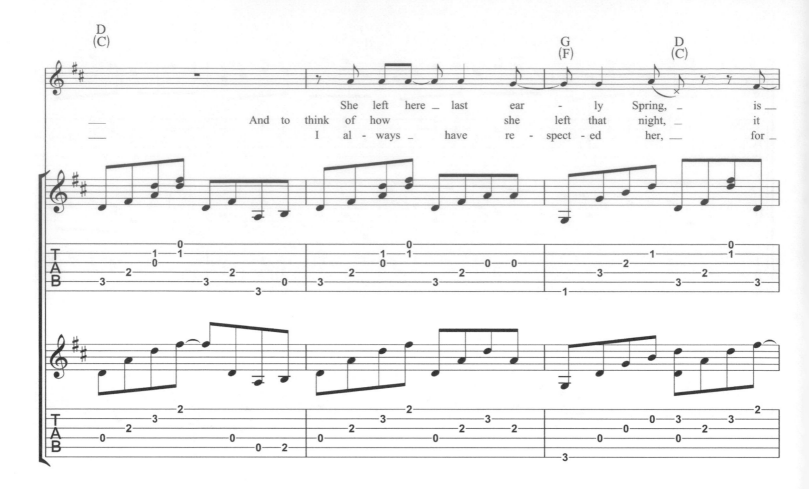

She left here _ last ear - ly Spring, _ is _
And to think of how she left that night, _ it
I al - ways _ have re - spect - ed her, _ for _

_ liv - in' there, I hear. _
still brings me a chill. _
_ bust - ing out _ and get - tin' free. _

And
Oh _

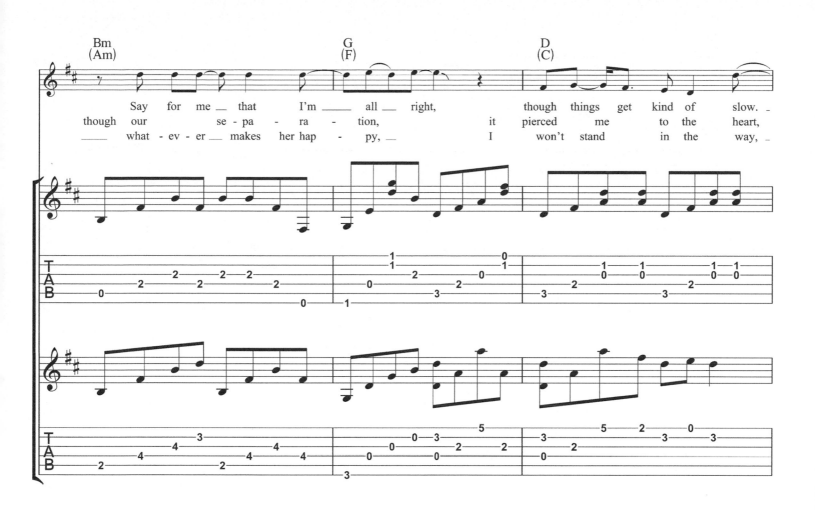

Say for me ___ that I'm ___ all ___ right, though things get kind of slow. ___
though our se - pa - ra - tion, it pierced me to the heart,
___ what - ev - er ___ makes her hap - py, ___ I won't stand in the way, ___

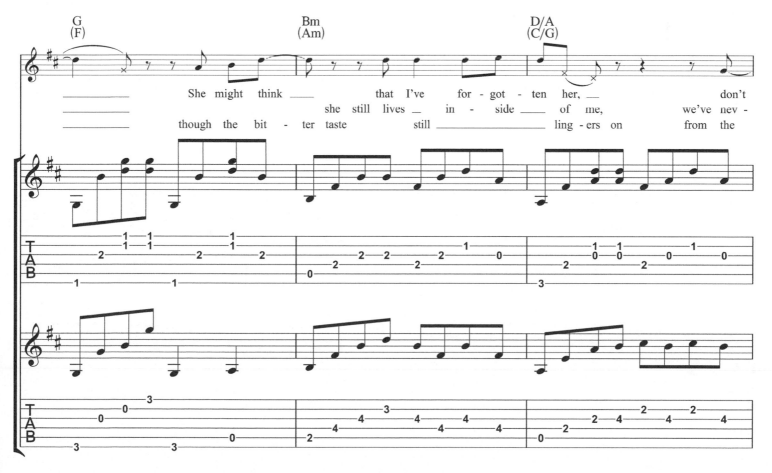

___ She might think ___ that I've for - got - ten her, ___ don't
___ she still lives ___ in - side ___ of me, we've nev -
___ though the bit - ter taste still ___ ling - ers on from the

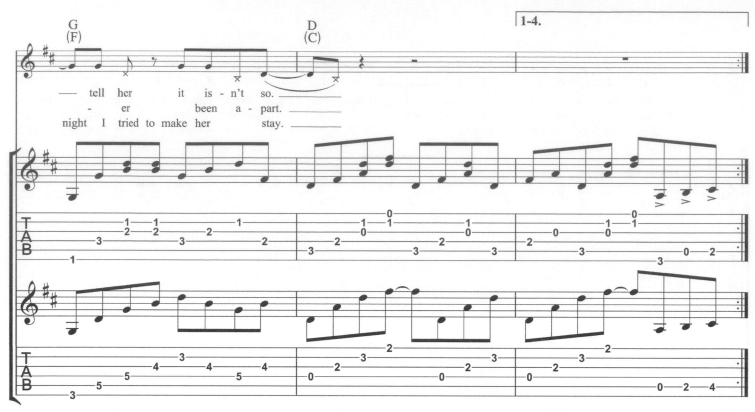

— tell her it is - n't so. _____
- er been a - part. _____
night I tried to make her stay. _____

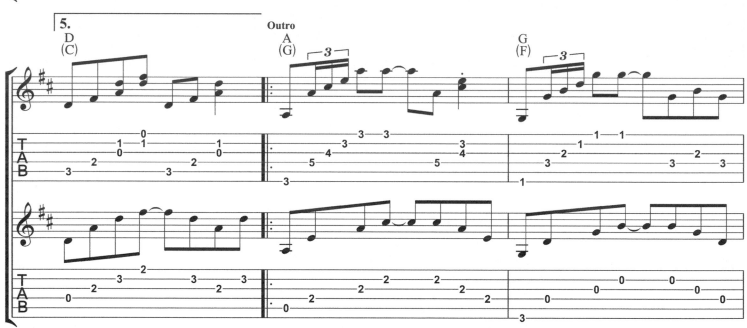

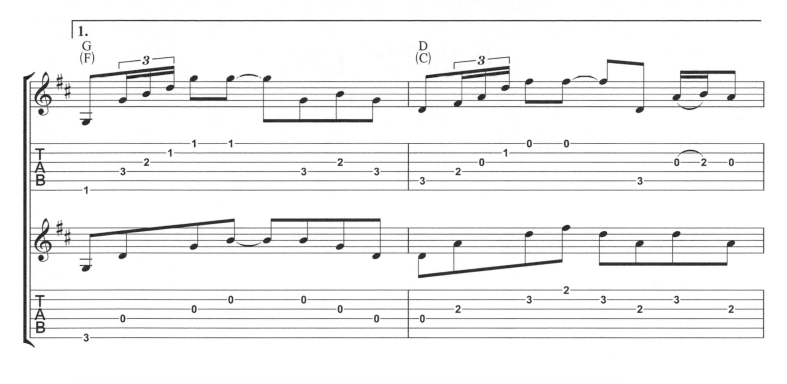

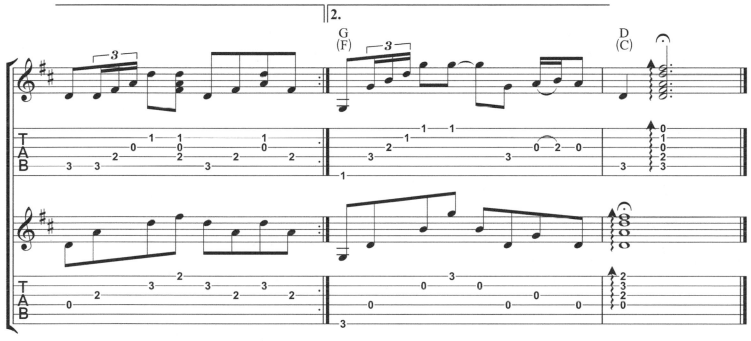

*Verse 4:*
I see a lot of people as I make the rounds
And I hear her name here and there as I go from town to town
And I've never gotten used to it, I've just learned to turn it off
Either I'm too sensitive or else I'm gettin' soft

*Verse 5:*
Sundown, yellow moon, I replay the past
I know every scene by heart, they all went by so fast
If she's passin' back this way, I'm not that hard to find
Tell her she can look me up if she's got the time

# IT AIN'T ME, BABE

**Words & Music by Bob Dylan**

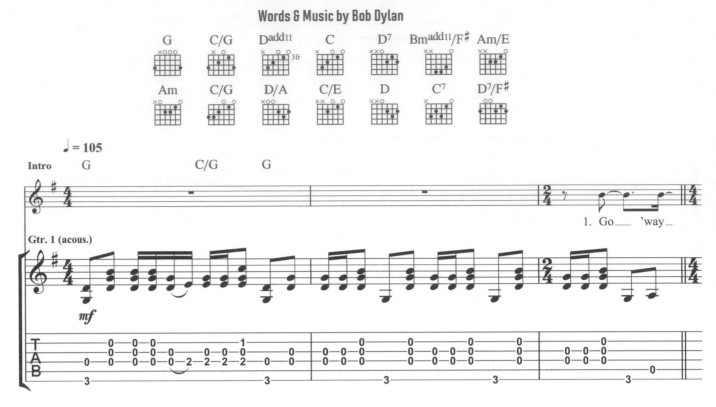

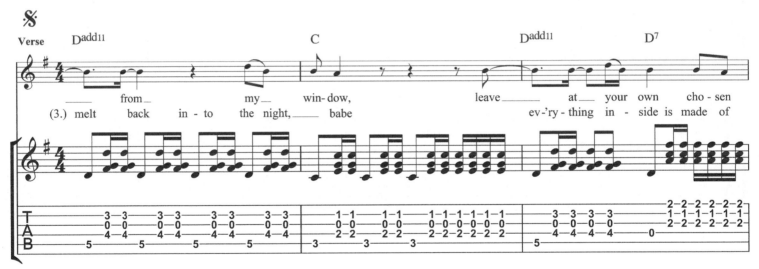

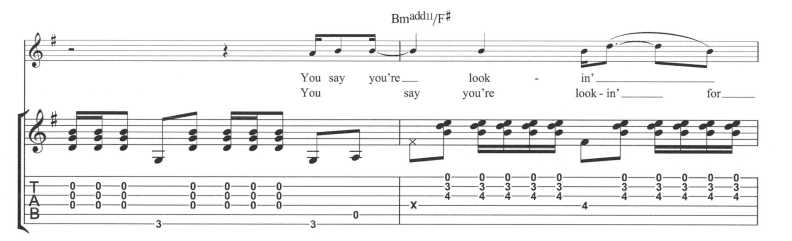

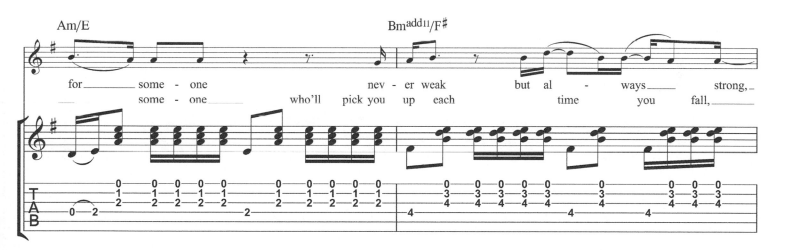

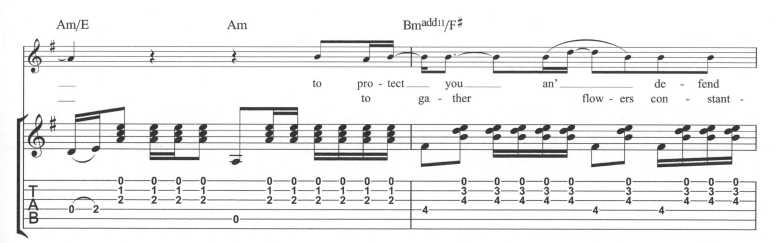

you    whe-ther you___ are    right_ or_    wrong,___      some - one
-ly    an' to come__ each    time_ you    call,___      a

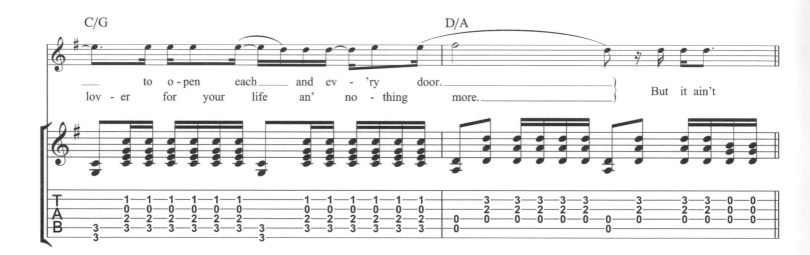

___   to o - pen each___ and ev - 'ry    door._____ But it ain't
lov - er   for your life an' no - thing    more._____

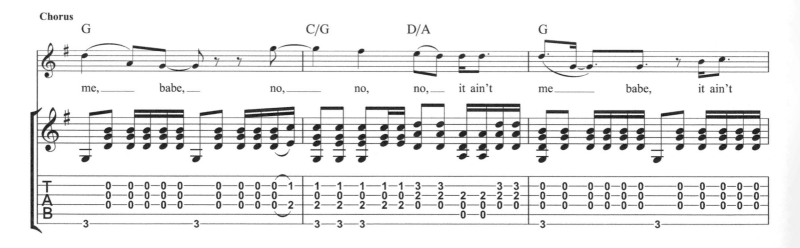

me,___ babe,___    no,___ no, no,___ it ain't    me___ babe,    it ain't

me you're look - in'_ for,___ babe.

68

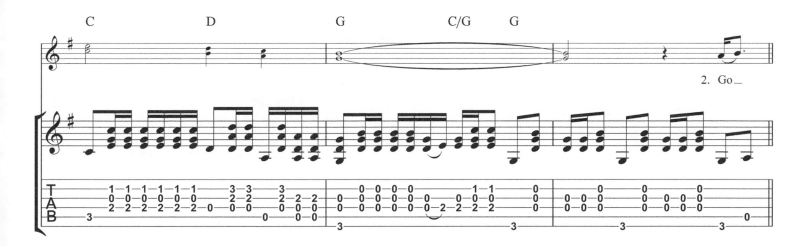

2. Go —

**Verse**

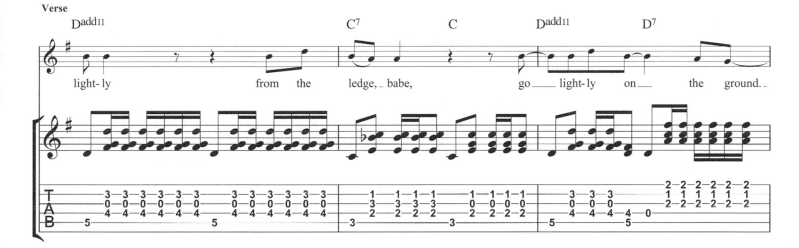

light-ly     from the ledge, _ babe,     go __ light-ly on __ the ground. _

__ I'm _ not the one you _ want, _

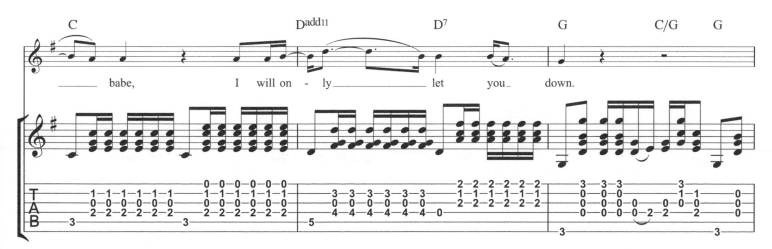

__ babe,     I will on - ly _____ let you _ down.

69

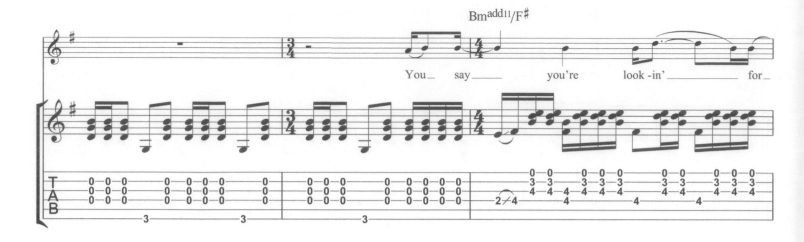

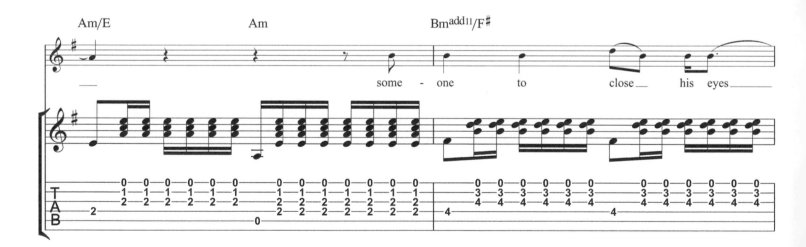

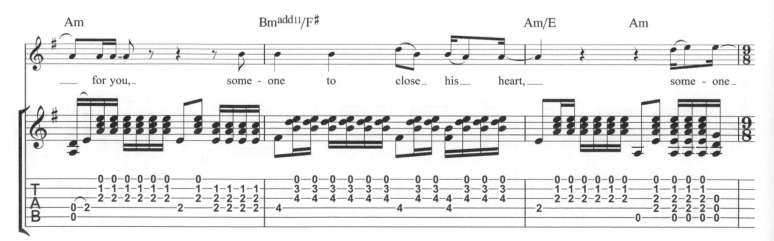

70

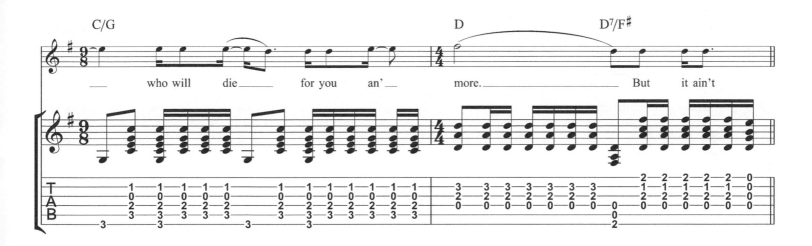

who will die____ for you an'____ more._____ But it ain't

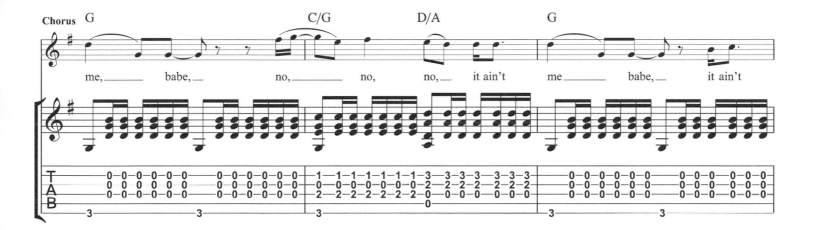

**Chorus** G ... C/G ... D/A ... G

me,____ babe,____ no,____ no,____ no,____ it ain't me____ babe,____ it ain't

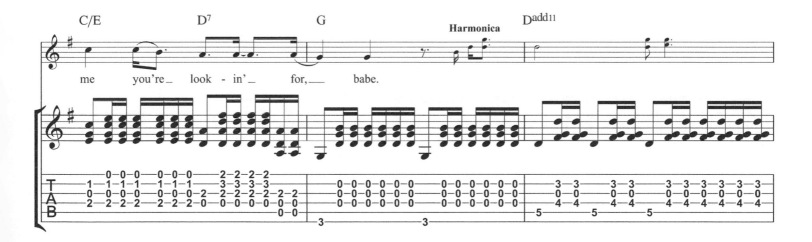

C/E ... D⁷ ... G ... **Harmonica** ... Dadd11

me you're____ look - in'____ for,____ babe.

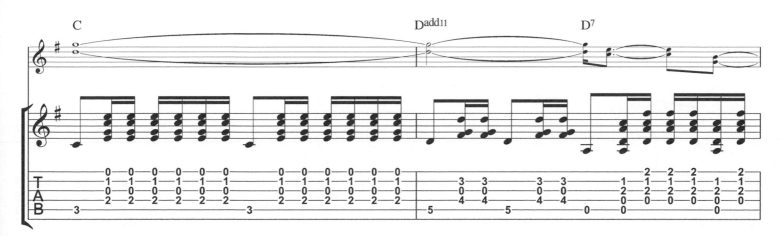

C ... Dadd11 ... D⁷

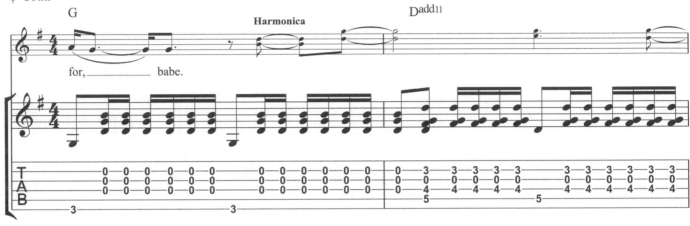

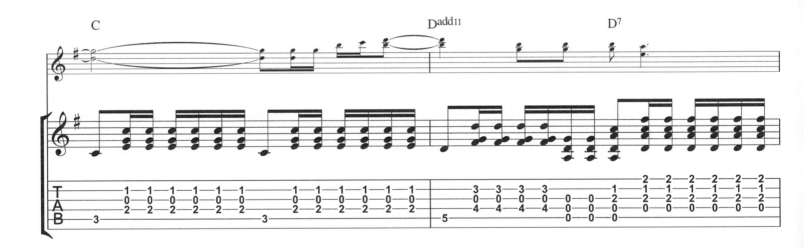

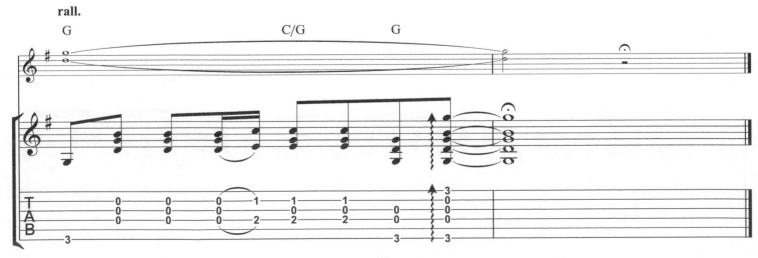

# LAY, LADY, LAY

Words & Music by Bob Dylan

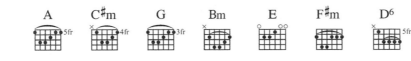

75

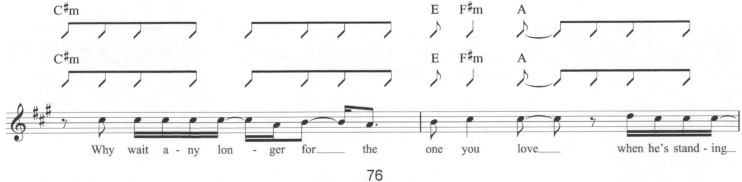

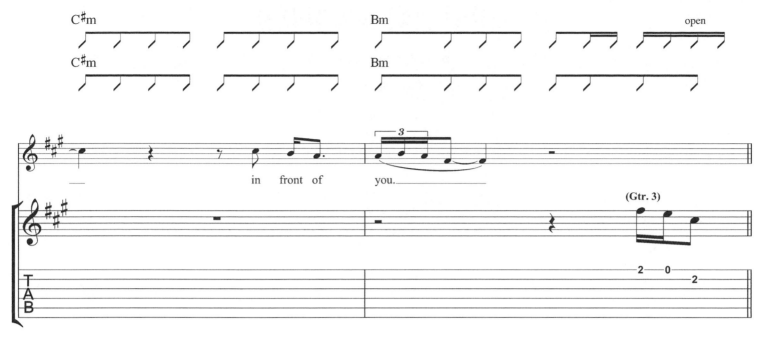

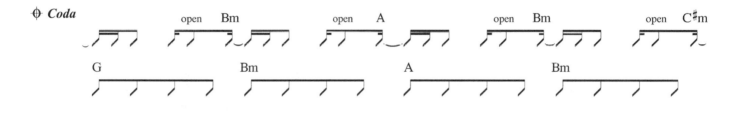

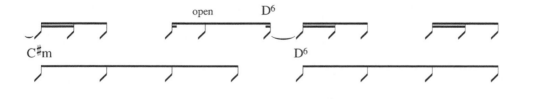

# JUST LIKE A WOMAN

**Words & Music by Bob Dylan**

†Symbols in parentheses represent chord names with respect to capoed guitar. (Tab 0 = 5 fret.) Symbols above represent actual sounding chords.

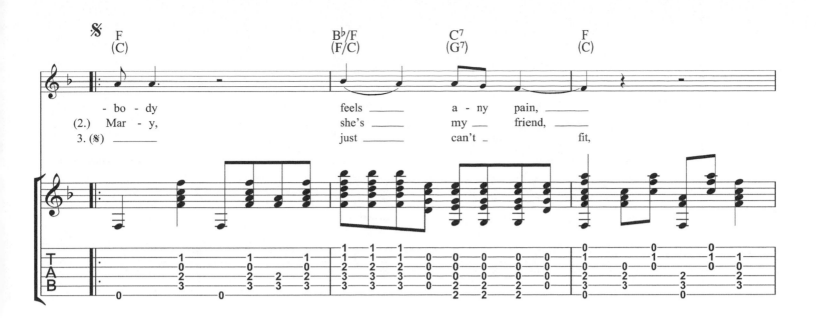

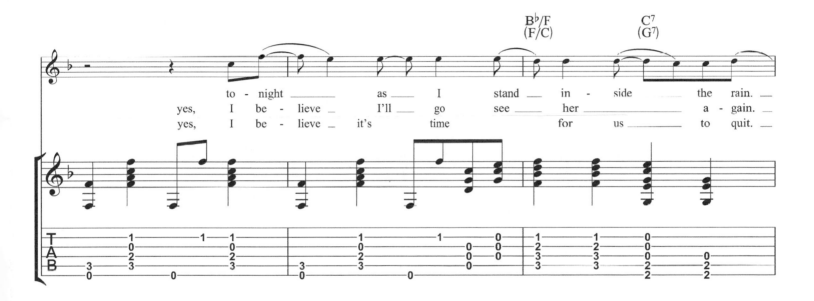

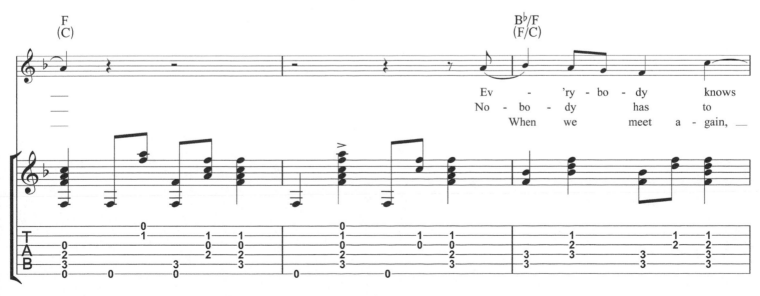

79

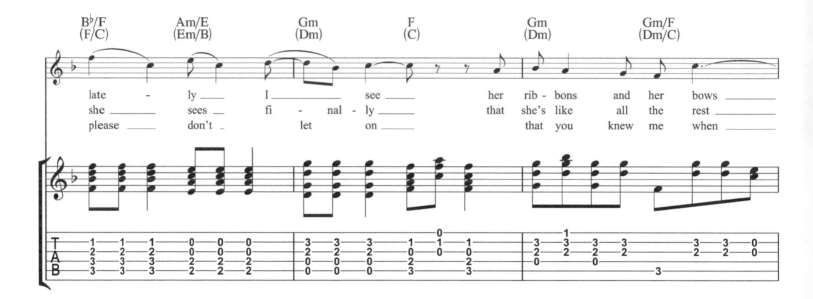

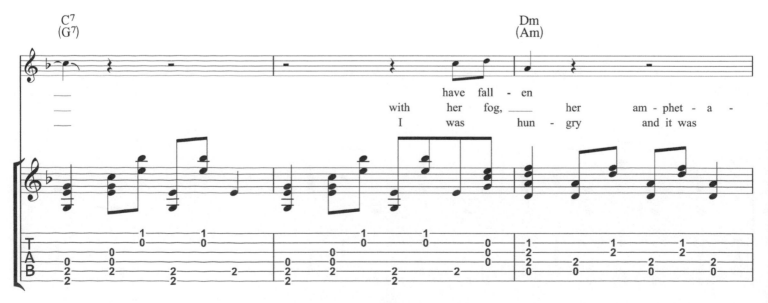

just like a lit - tle girl. ___
just like a lit - tle girl. ___

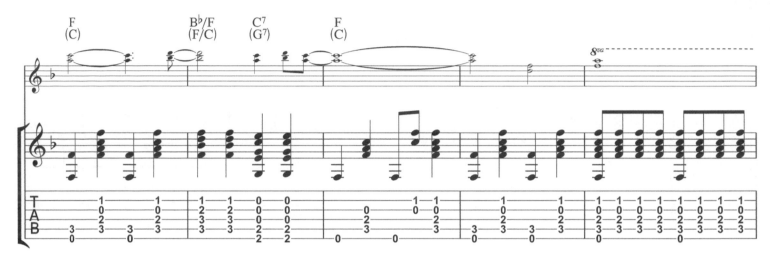

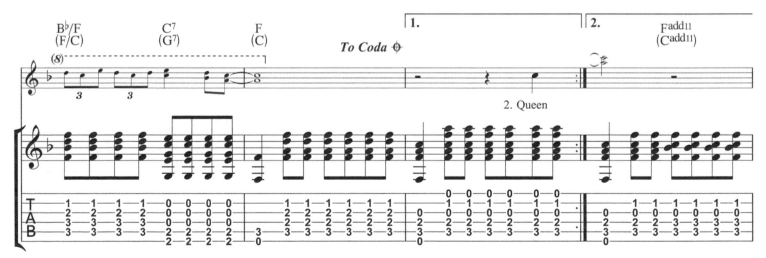

2. Queen

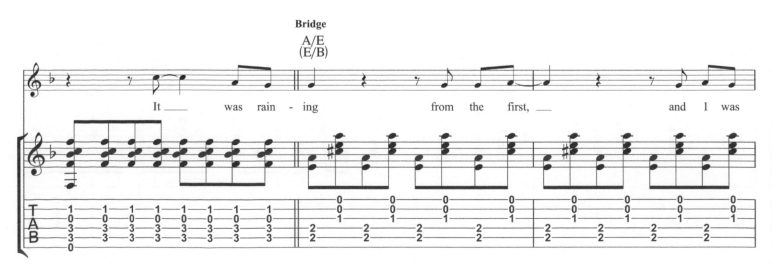

**Bridge**

It ___ was rain - ing from the first, ___ and I was

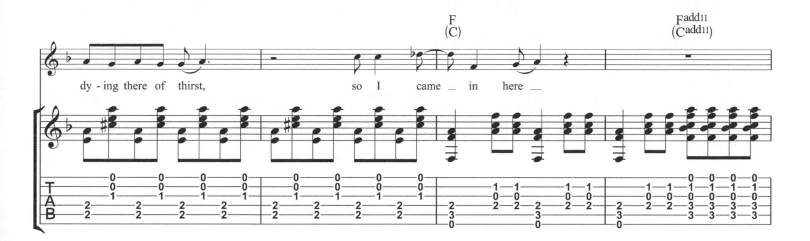

dy - ing there of thirst, so I came _ in here _

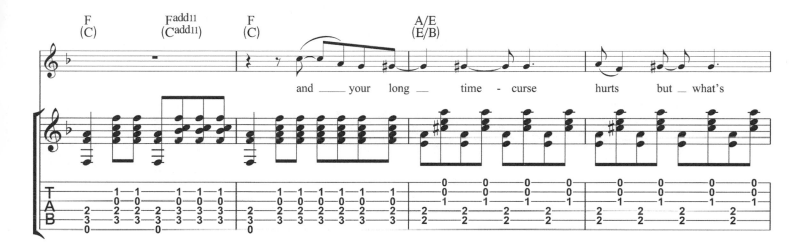

and _ your long _ time - curse hurts but _ what's

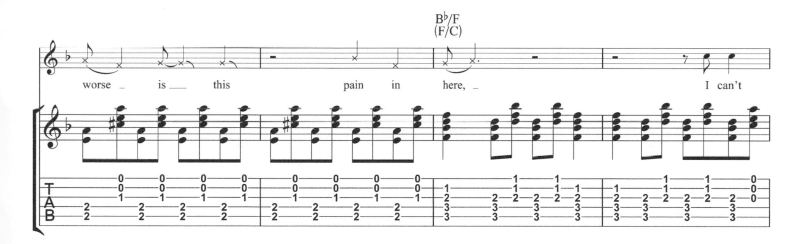

worse _ is _ this pain in here, _ I can't

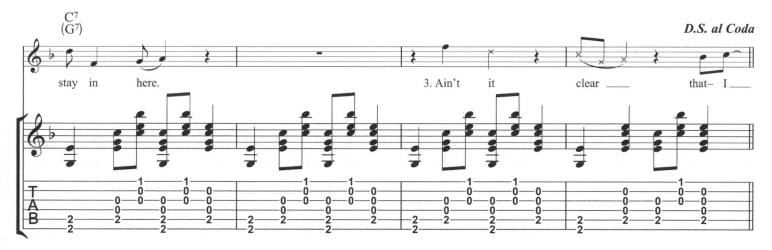

stay in here. 3. Ain't it clear ___ that— I ___

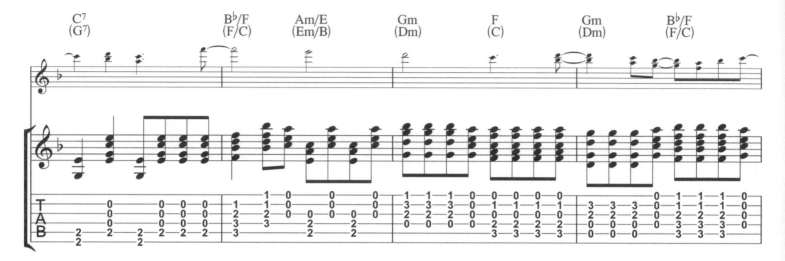

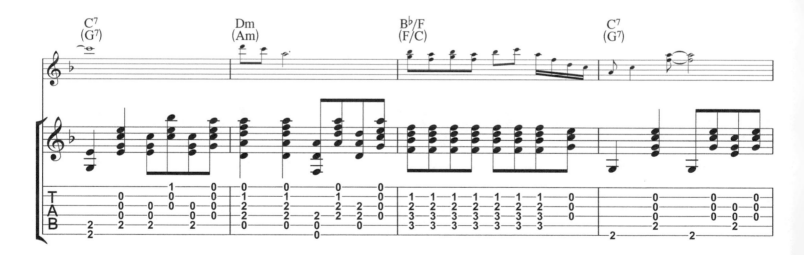

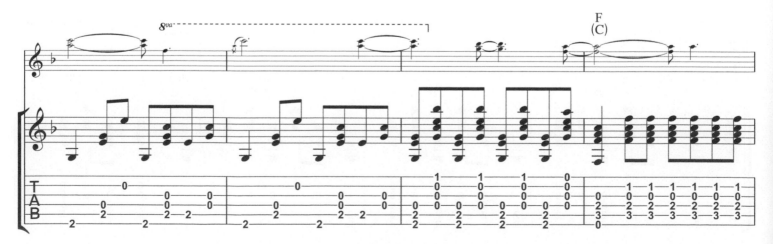

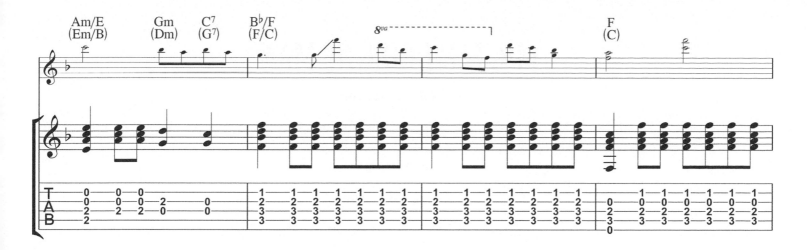

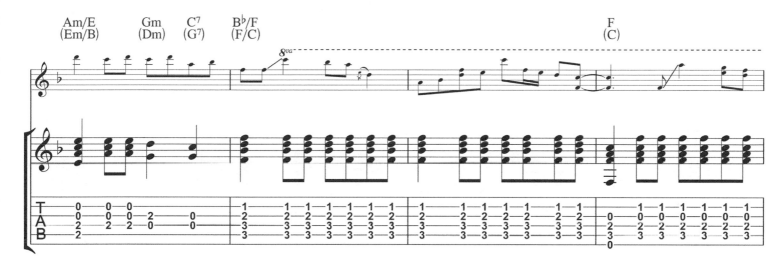

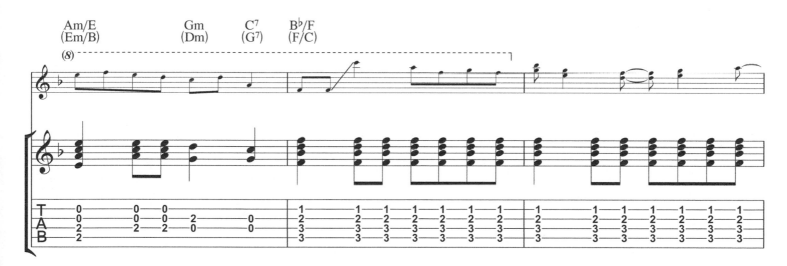

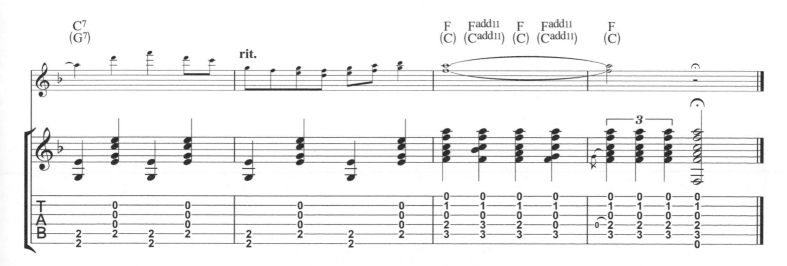

# MR. TAMBOURINE MAN

Words & Music by Bob Dylan

†Symbols in parentheses represent chord names with respect to capoed guitar. (Tab 0 = 3 fret.)
Symbols above represent actual sounding chords.

**Verse**

that eve-nin's em - pire has re-turned in-to sand, van-ished from my

hand, left me blind - ly here to stand but still not sleep - ing. My

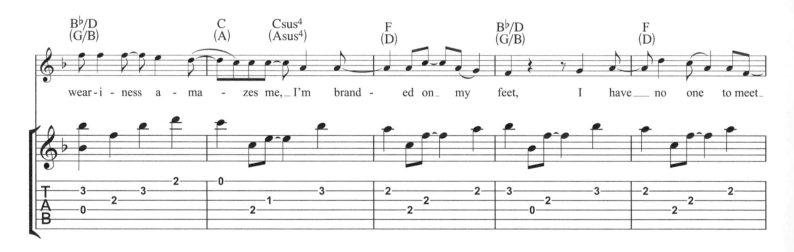

wear-i - ness a - ma - zes me, I'm brand - ed on my feet, I have no one to meet

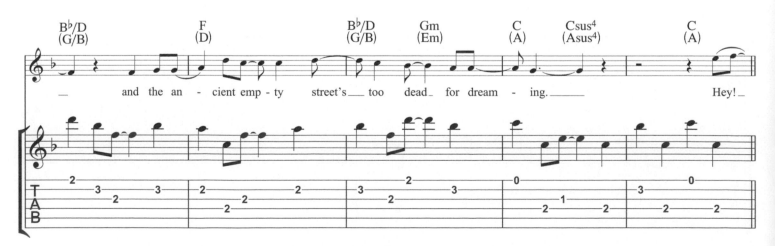

and the an - cient emp-ty street's too dead for dream - ing. Hey!

**Chorus**

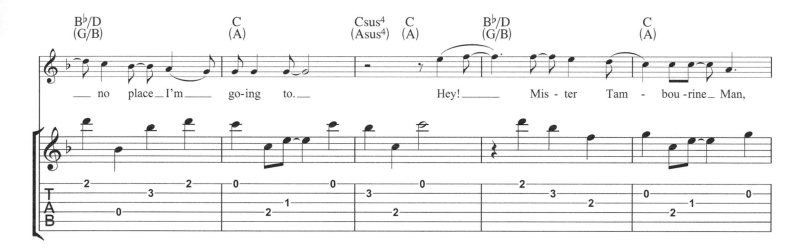

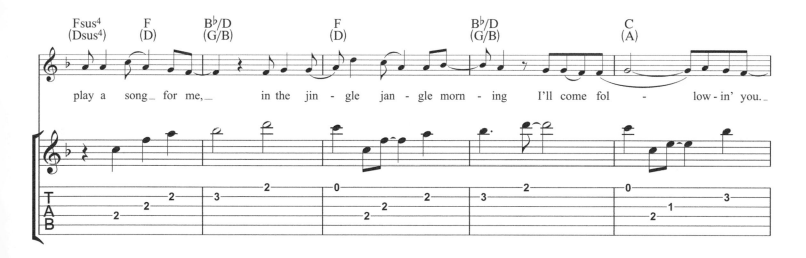

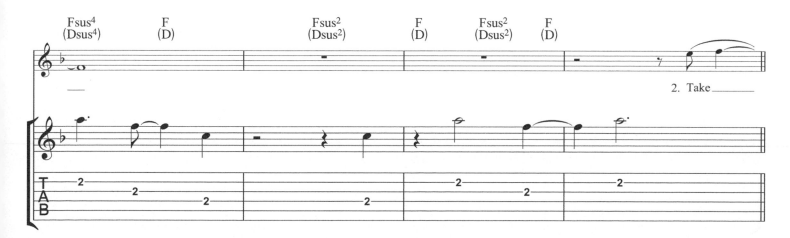

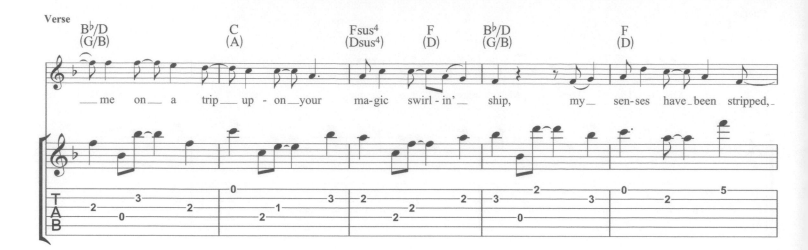

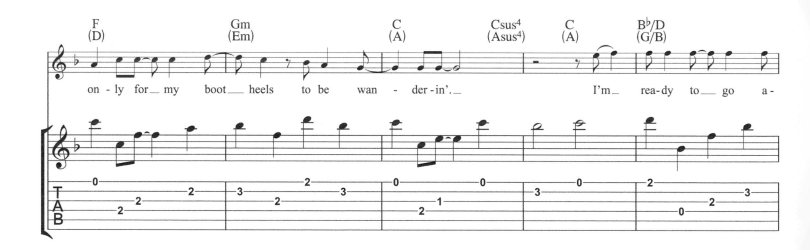

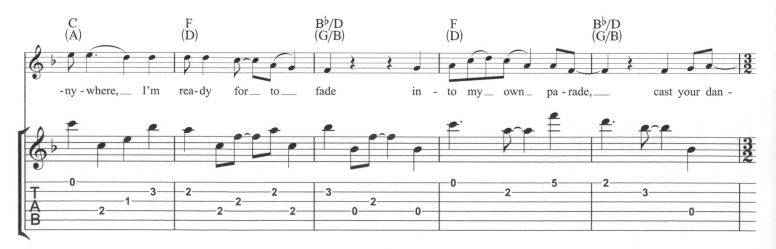

90

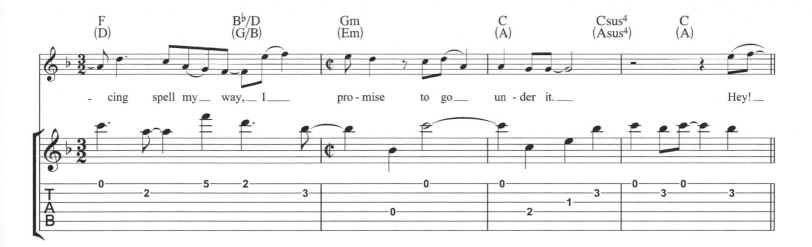

-cing spell my\_ way,\_ I\_ pro - mise to go\_ un - der it.\_ Hey!\_

**Chorus**

\_ Mis - ter Tam - bou -rine\_ Man,\_ play a song\_ for me,\_ I'm not sleep - y and there is\_

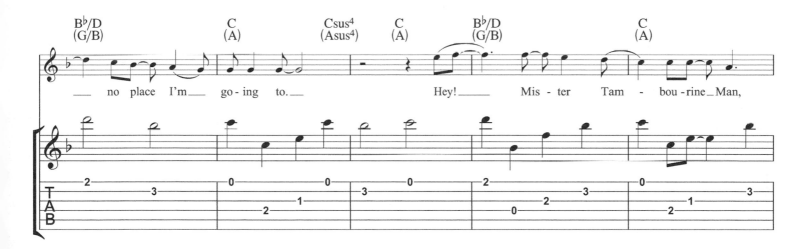

\_ no place I'm\_ go - ing to.\_ Hey!\_ Mis - ter Tam - bou -rine\_ Man,

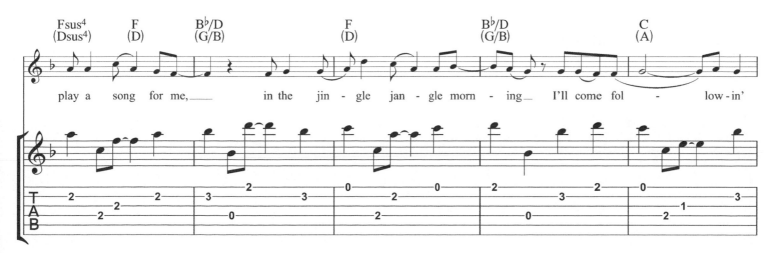

play a song\_ for me,\_ in the jin - gle jan - gle morn - ing\_ I'll come fol - low -in'

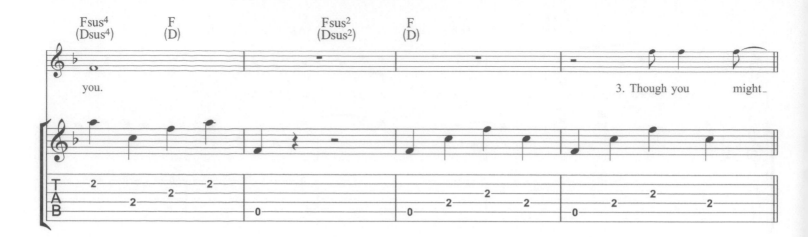

you.  3. Though you might

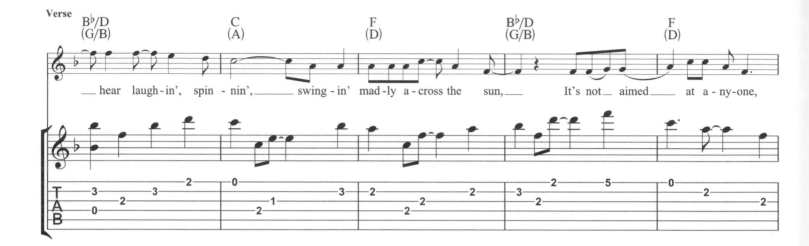

Verse

— hear laugh-in', spin - nin',___ swing-in' mad-ly a-cross the  sun,___ It's not___ aimed___ at a - ny-one,

it's just es - cap - in' on___ the run___ and but  for___ the  sky__ there are___ no__ fen-ces

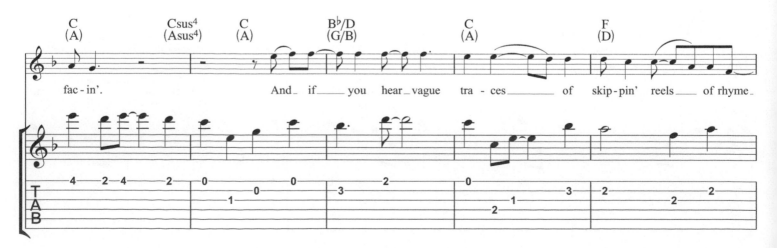

fac - in'.  And__ if___ you  hear__ vague  tra - ces___ of  skip-pin'  reels__ of rhyme__

92

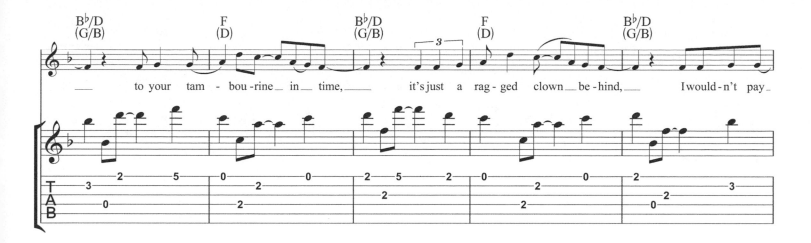

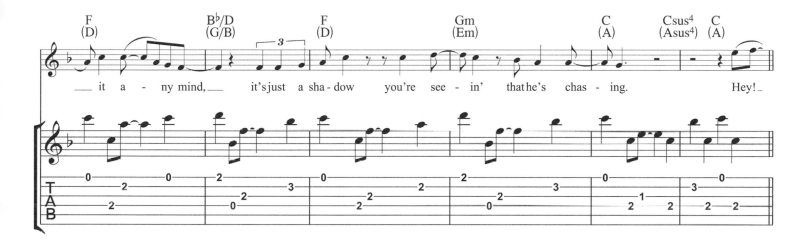

**Chorus**

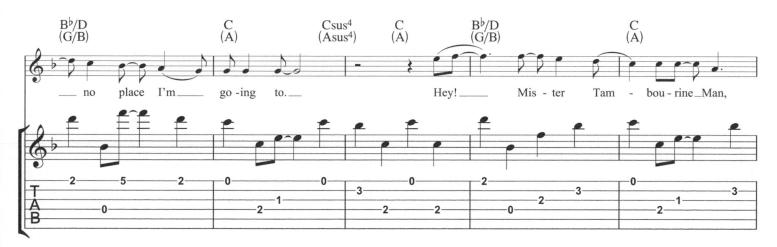

93

play a    song  for me,____    in the  jin - gle  jan-gle morn-ing   I'll come fol - low-in' you.__

**Harmonica solo**

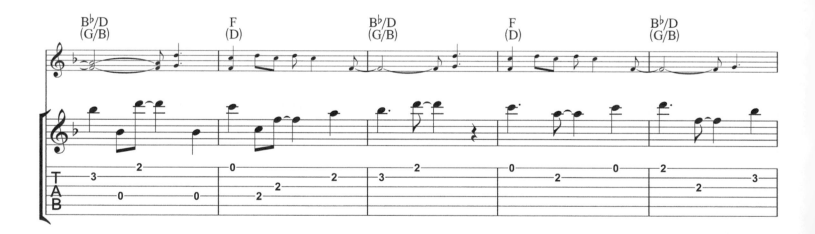

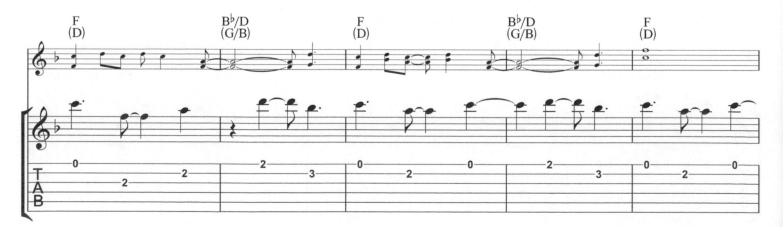

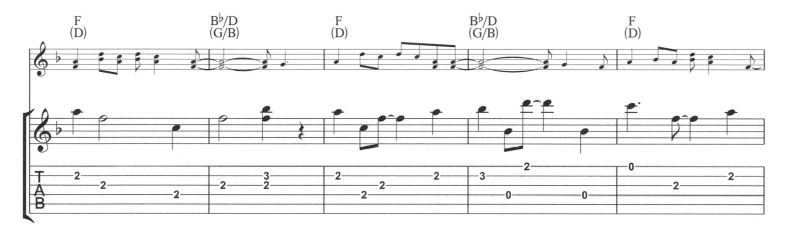

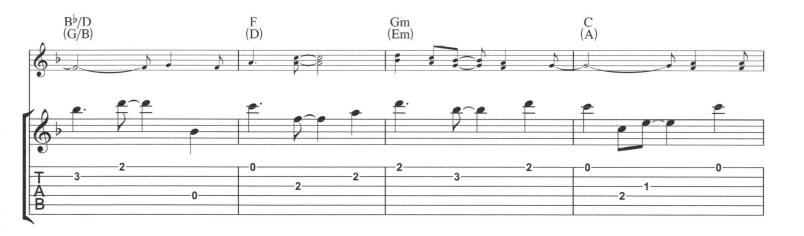

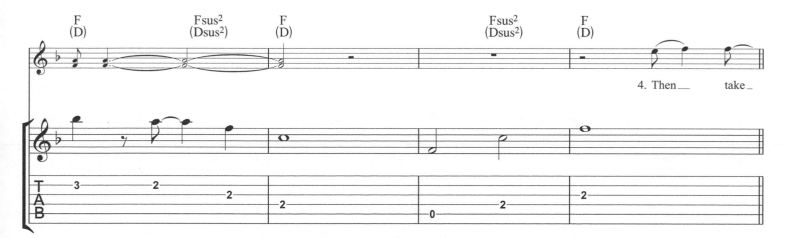

4. Then____ take____

**Verse**

\_\_ me dis - ap - pear - in' through the smoke\_\_ rings of\_\_ my\_\_ mind,\_\_ down the fog-

- gy ru - ins of time, \_\_ far past\_\_ the fro - zen leaves, \_\_ the haunt- ed, fright- ened trees, \_\_

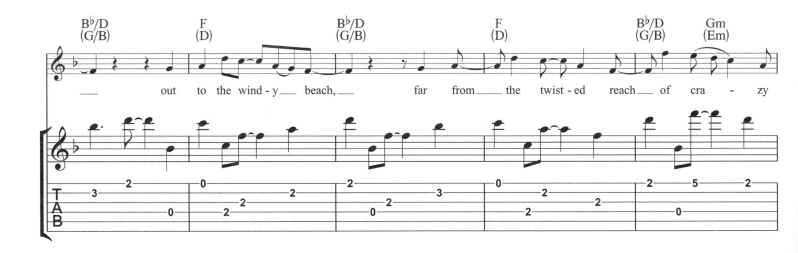

\_\_ out to the wind - y beach, \_\_ far from\_\_ the twist - ed reach\_\_ of cra - zy

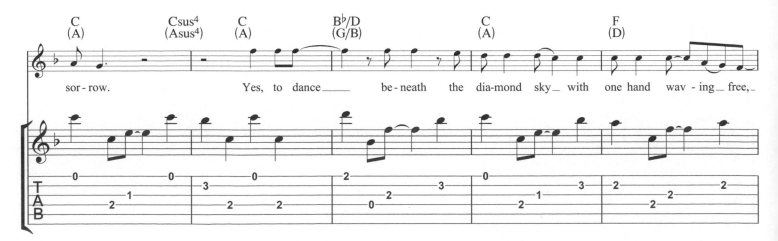

sor - row. Yes, to dance\_\_ be - neath the dia - mond sky\_\_ with one hand wav - ing\_\_ free, \_\_

96

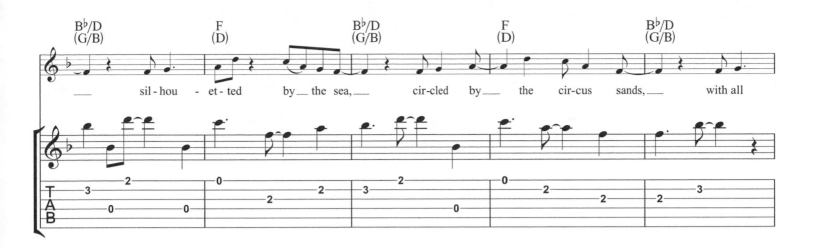

silhou - et - ted by the sea, cir - cled by the cir - cus sands, with all

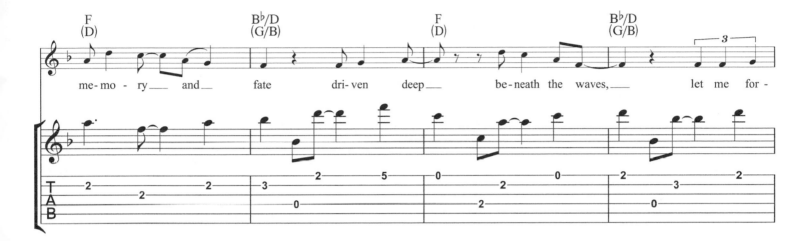

me - mo - ry and fate dri - ven deep be - neath the waves, let me for -

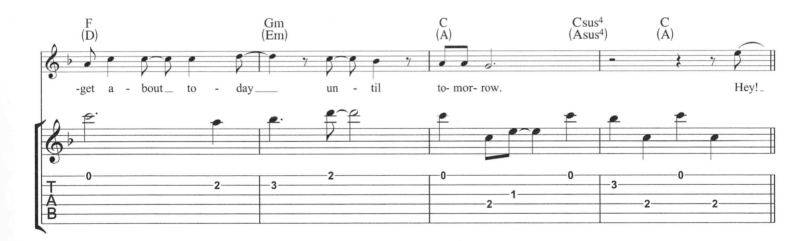

-get a - bout to - day un - til to - mor - row. Hey!

**Chorus**

Mis - ter Tam - bou - rine Man, play a song for me, I'm not sleep - y and there is

— no place I'm\_ go-ing to.\_\_     Hey!\_\_ Mis - ter Tam - bou-rine\_ Man,

play a song\_for me,\_\_    in the jin - gle jan-gle morn - ing I'll come fol - low-in' you.\_\_

**Harmonica solo**

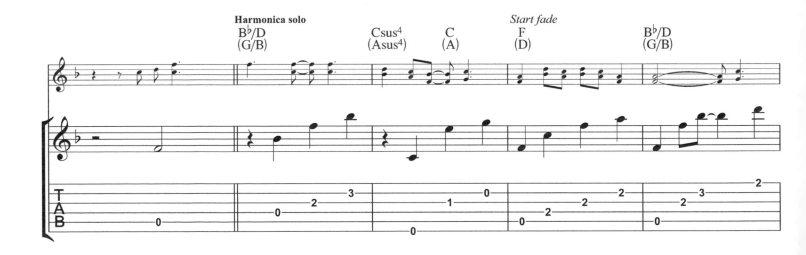

*Start fade*

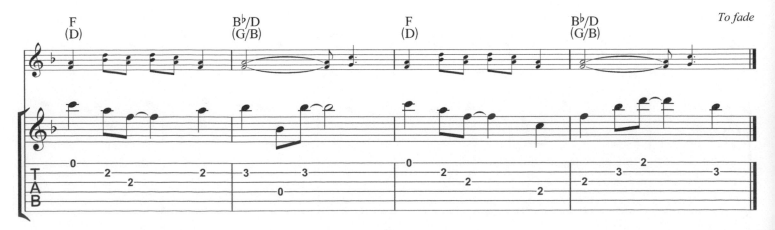

*To fade*

98

# SHOOTING STAR

**Words & Music by Bob Dylan**

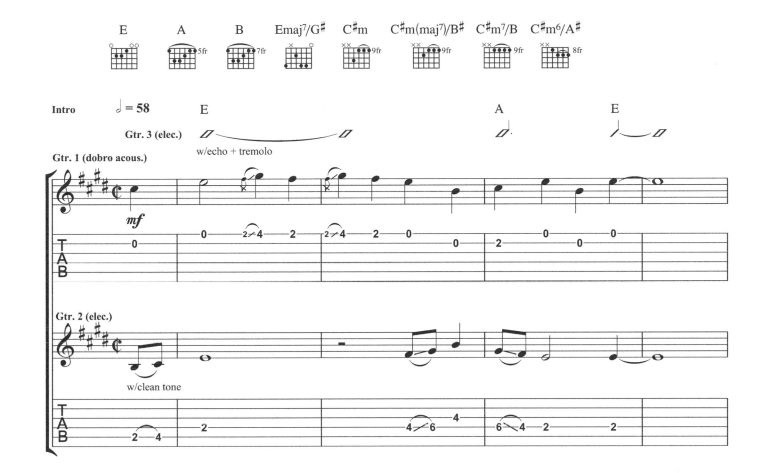

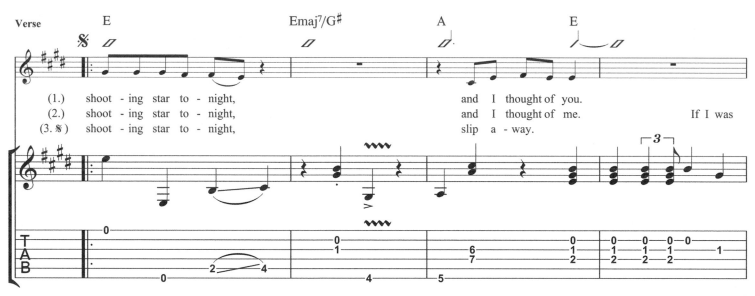

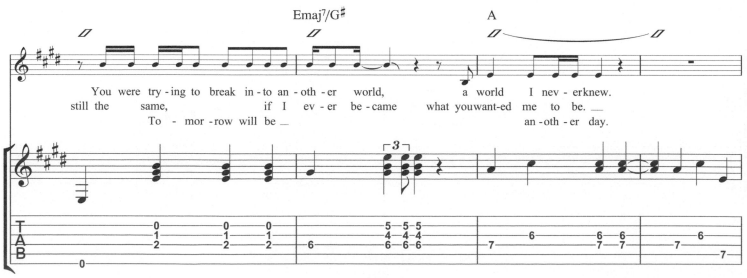

100

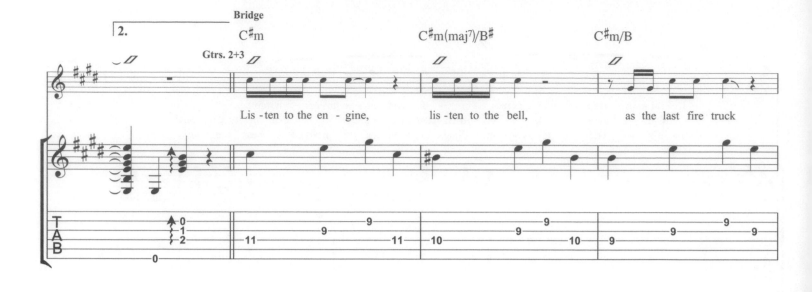

Lis -ten to the en - gine, lis -ten to the bell, as the last fire truck

from hell __ goes roll -ing by, all good peo -ple are pray -ing.

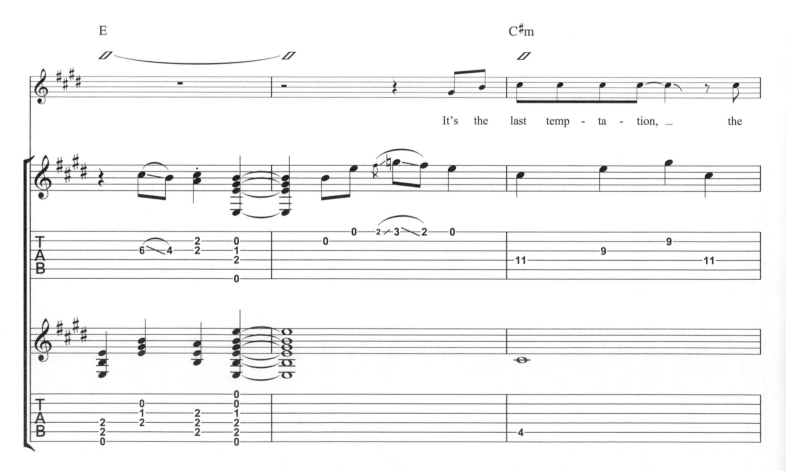

It's the last temp - ta - tion, __ the

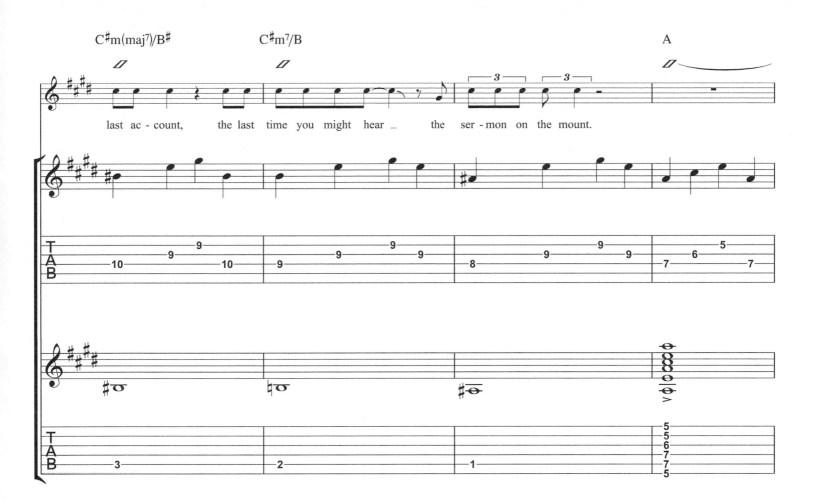

last ac - count, the last time you might hear _ the ser - mon on the mount.

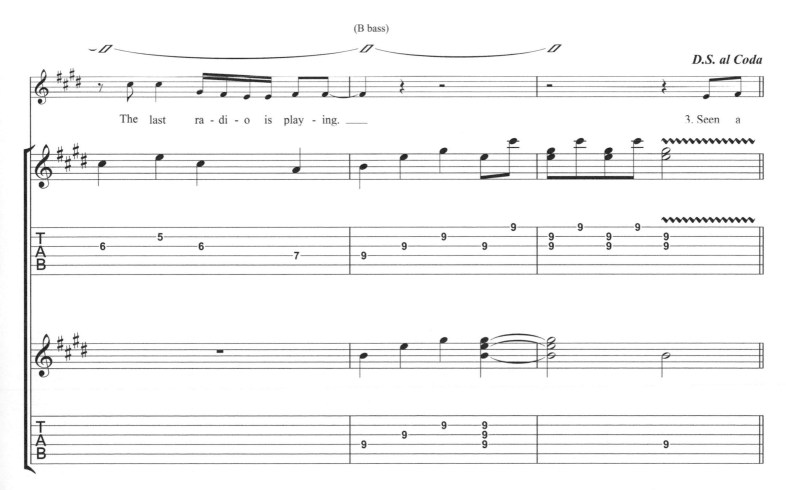

The last ra - di - o is play - ing. ____ 3. Seen a

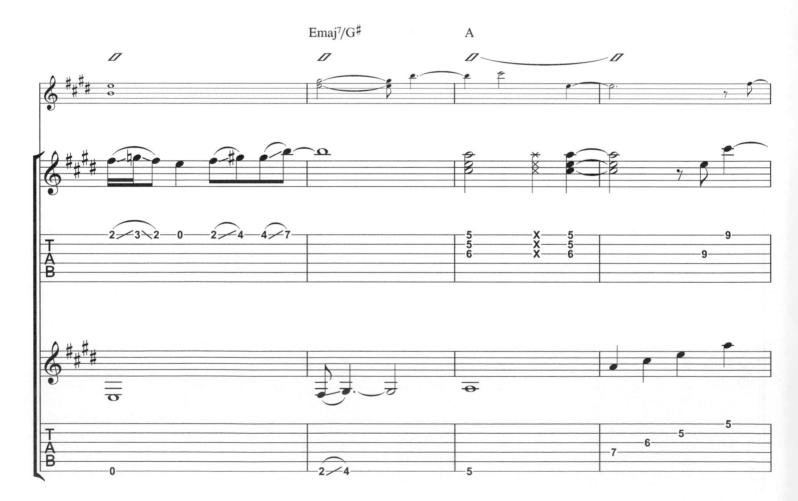

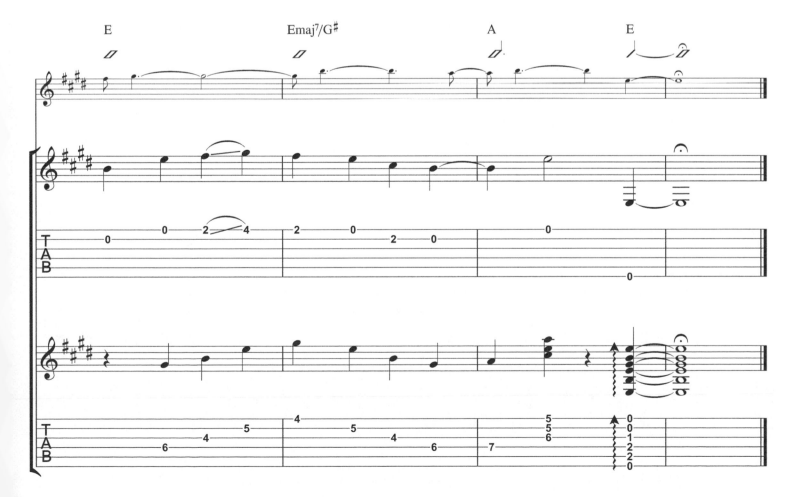

# MASTERS OF WAR

### Words & Music by Bob Dylan

†Symbols in parentheses represent chord names with respect to capoed guitar. (Tab 0 = 3 fret.) Symbols above represent actual sounding chords.

109

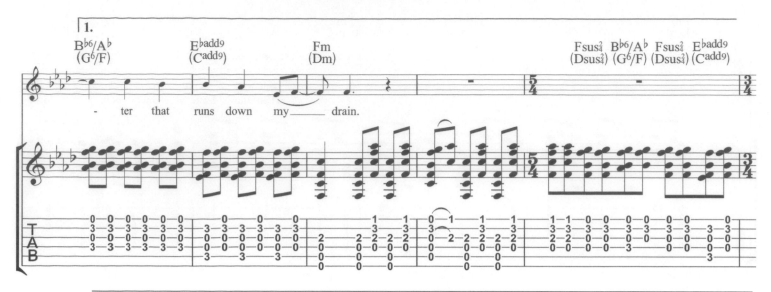

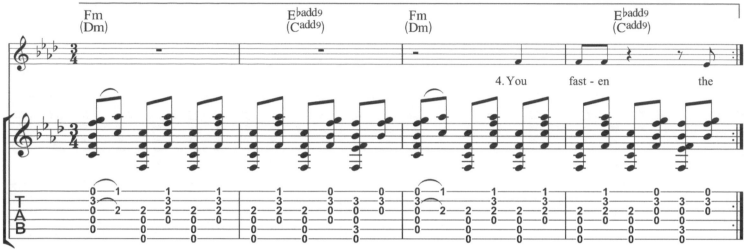

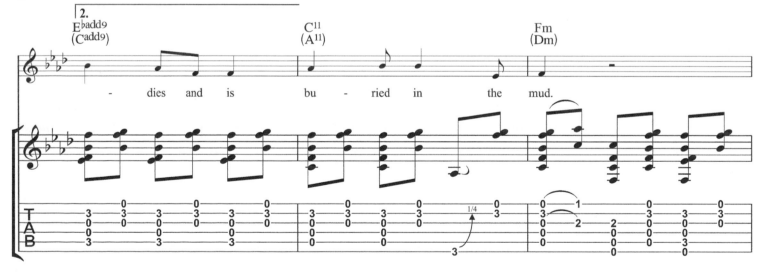

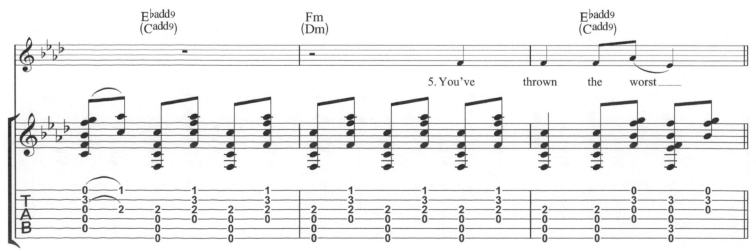

Fm (Dm)     E♭add9 (Cadd9)     Fm (Dm)     E♭add9 (Cadd9)     B♭6/D (G6/B)

- by,
know,     un - born and un -
though I'm young - er than___

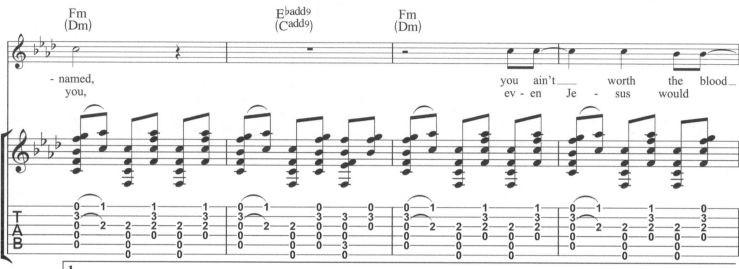

Fm (Dm)     E♭add9 (Cadd9)     Fm (Dm)

- named,
you,     you ain't___ worth the blood___
ev - en Je - sus would

**1.**

E♭add9 (Cadd9)     Fm (Dm)

___ that runs___ in your veins. ___

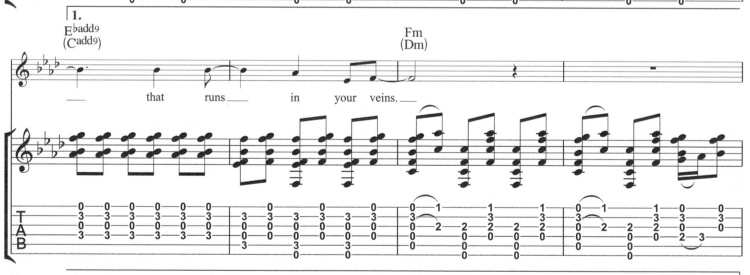

Fm (Dm)     E♭add9 (Cadd9)     Fm (Dm)     E♭add9 (Cadd9)

6. How much do I know

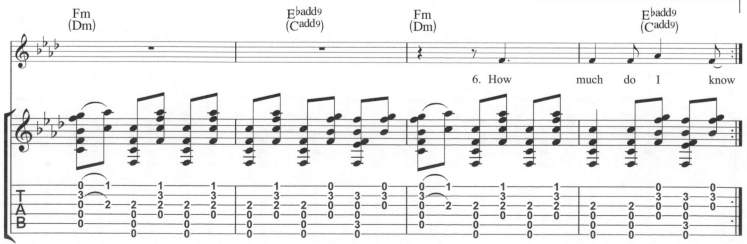

112

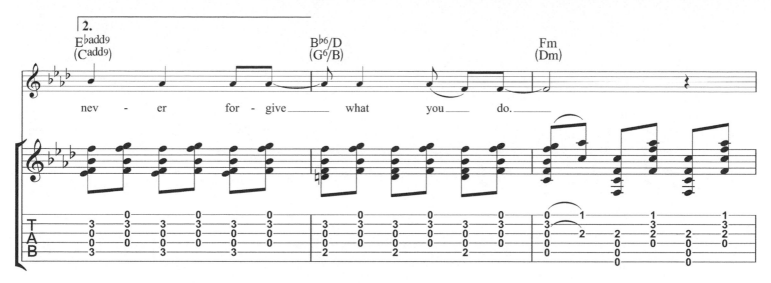

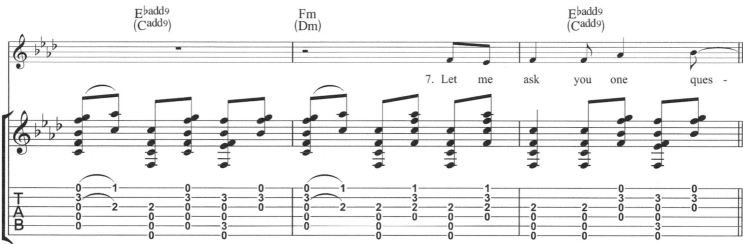

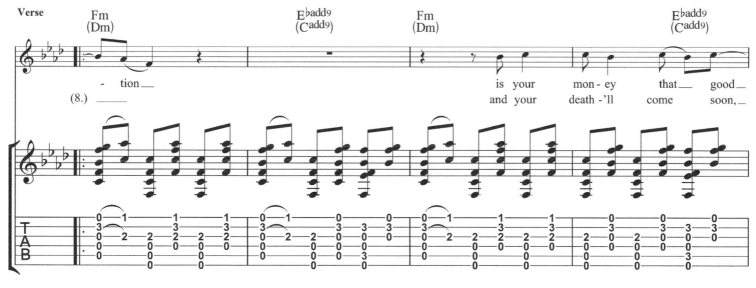

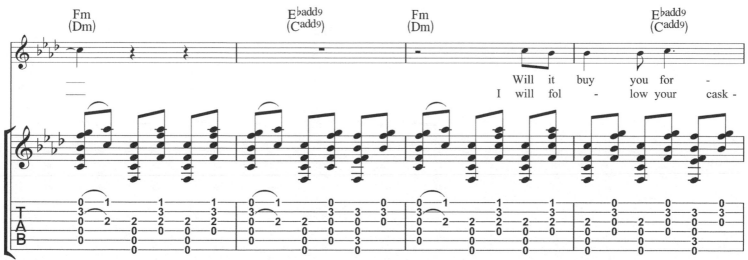

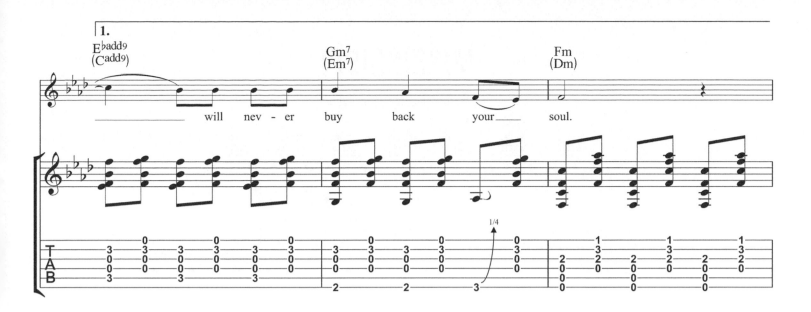

will nev - er buy back your soul.

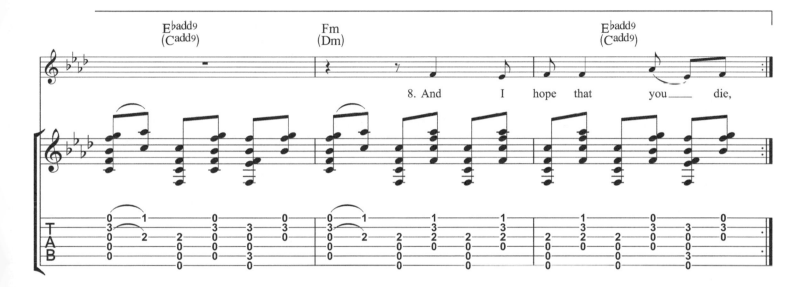

8. And I hope that you___ die,

grave 'til I'm sure that you're___ dead.

# MISSISSIPPI

### Words & Music by Bob Dylan

Got no-thin' for you,　　I had no-thin' be-fore,　　don't ev-en have an-y-thing for my-self
Some peo-ple will of-fer you their hand　and some won't,　last night I knew you, to-night

w/echo　　　let ring...

___ an-y-more.　　Sky full of fire,　　pain pour-in' down,___
___ I___ don't.　　I need some-thin' strong　to dis-tract my mind,　I'm

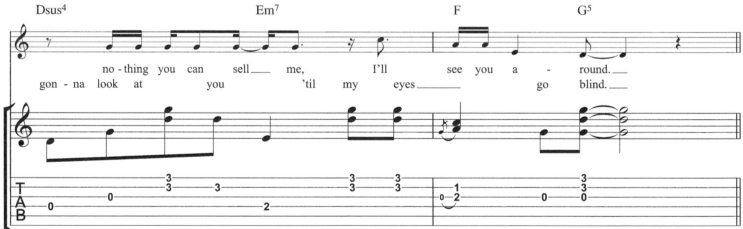

no-thing you can sell___ me,　I'll see you a-round.___
gon-na look at you　　'til my eyes___ go blind.___

**Chorus**

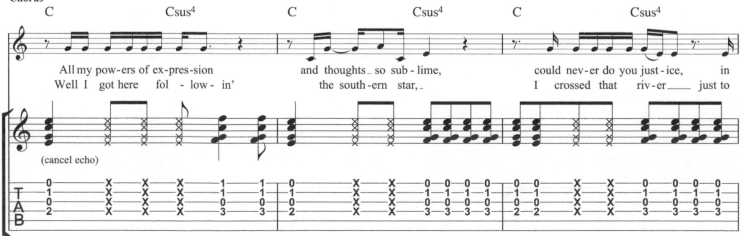

All my pow-ers of ex-pres-sion　　and thoughts so sub-lime,　　could nev-er do you just-ice,　in
Well I got here fol-low-in'　　the south-ern star,___　I crossed that riv-er___ just to

(cancel echo)

118

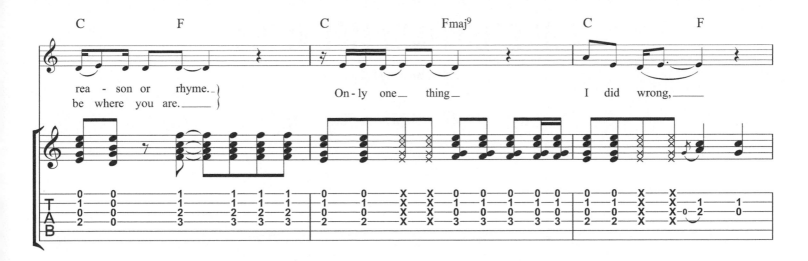

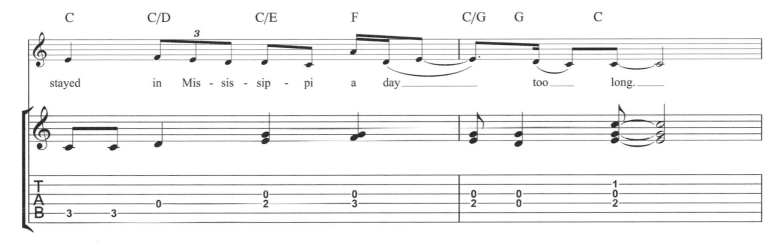

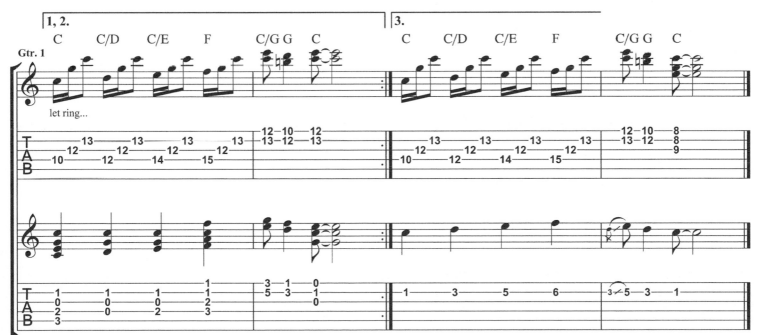

*Verse 3:*

Well my ship's been split to splinters and it's sinkin' fast
I'm drownin' in the poison, got no future, got no past
But my heart is not weary, it's light and it's free
I've got nothin' but affection for all those who've sailed with me

Everybody movin' if they ain't already there
Everybody got to move somewhere
Stick with me baby, stick with me anyhow
Things should start to get interesting right about now

My clothes are wet, tight on my skin
Not as tight as the corner that I painted myself in
I know that fortune is waitin' to be kind
So give me your hand and say you'll be mine

Well, the emptiness is endless, cold as the clay
You can always come back, but you can't come back all the way
Only one thing I did wrong
Stayed in Mississippi a day too long

# ONE TOO MANY MORNINGS

Words & Music by Bob Dylan

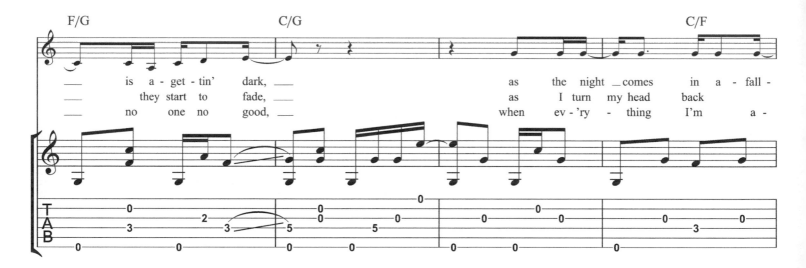

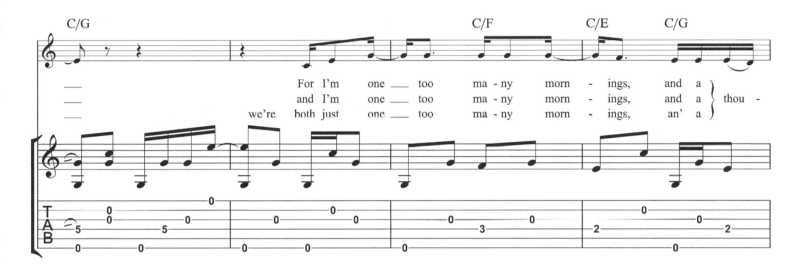

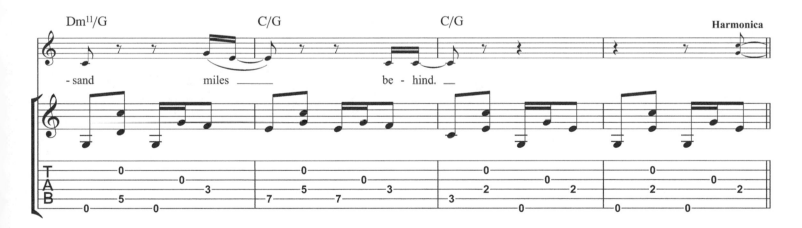

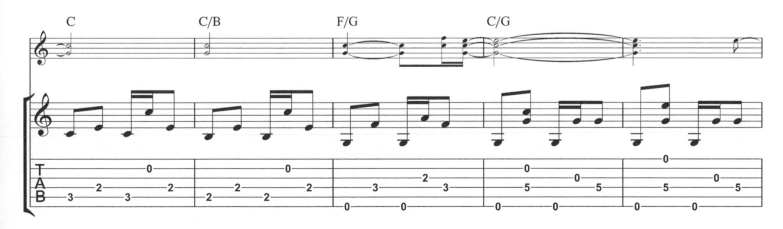

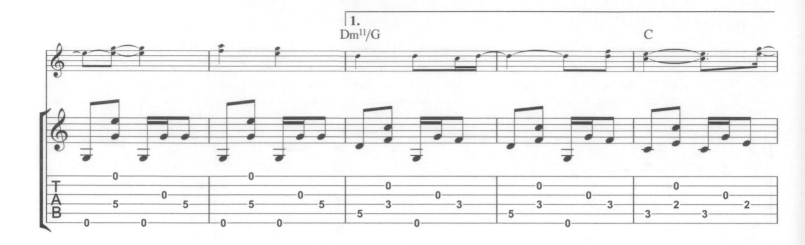

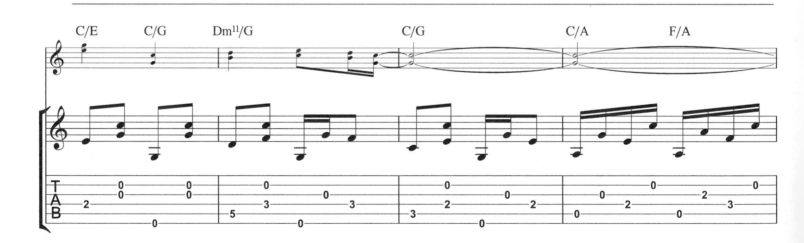

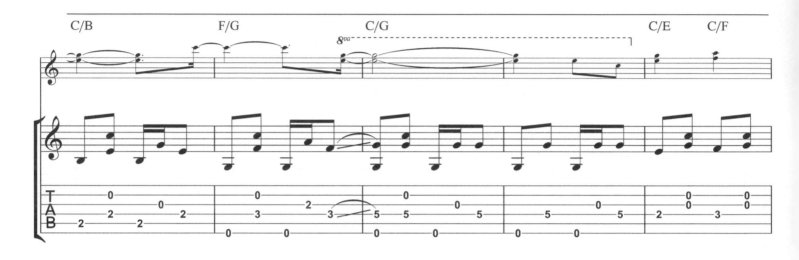

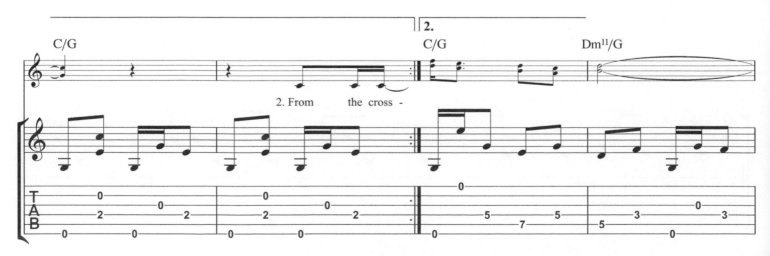

2. From    the  cross -

122

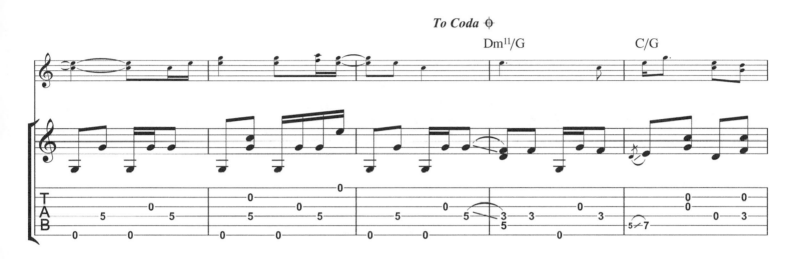

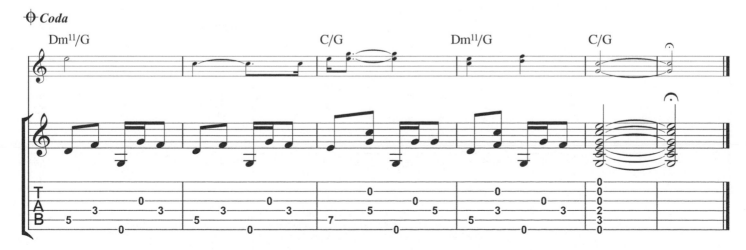

123

# VISIONS OF JOHANNA

**Words & Music by Bob Dylan**

†Symbols in parentheses represent chord names with respect to capoed guitar. (Tab 0 = 2 fr.) Symbols above represent actual sounding chords.

1. Ain't__ it just like the night__ to play tricks when you're try - in' to be so qui-

*(Verses 2-4 see block lyrics)*

holds a hand-ful of rain,     tempt-in' you to de-fy it.

Lights     flick-er from the op - po - site loft,___     in this

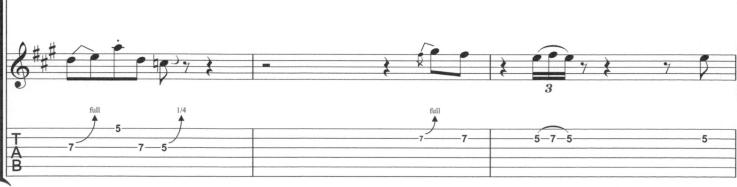

room　the heat pipes just　cough.　　　　The coun-try mu - sic sta - tion plays soft

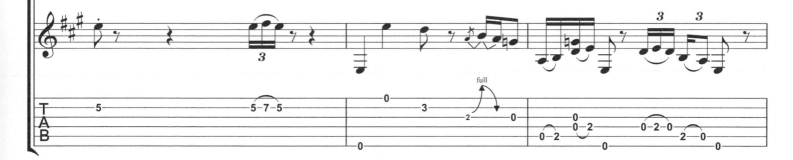

but there's no-thing, real-ly no-thing　to turn　off.　　　　Just　Lou-

-ise___ and her lo - ver so___ en - twined

and these vi - sions___ of Jo - han - na___ that___

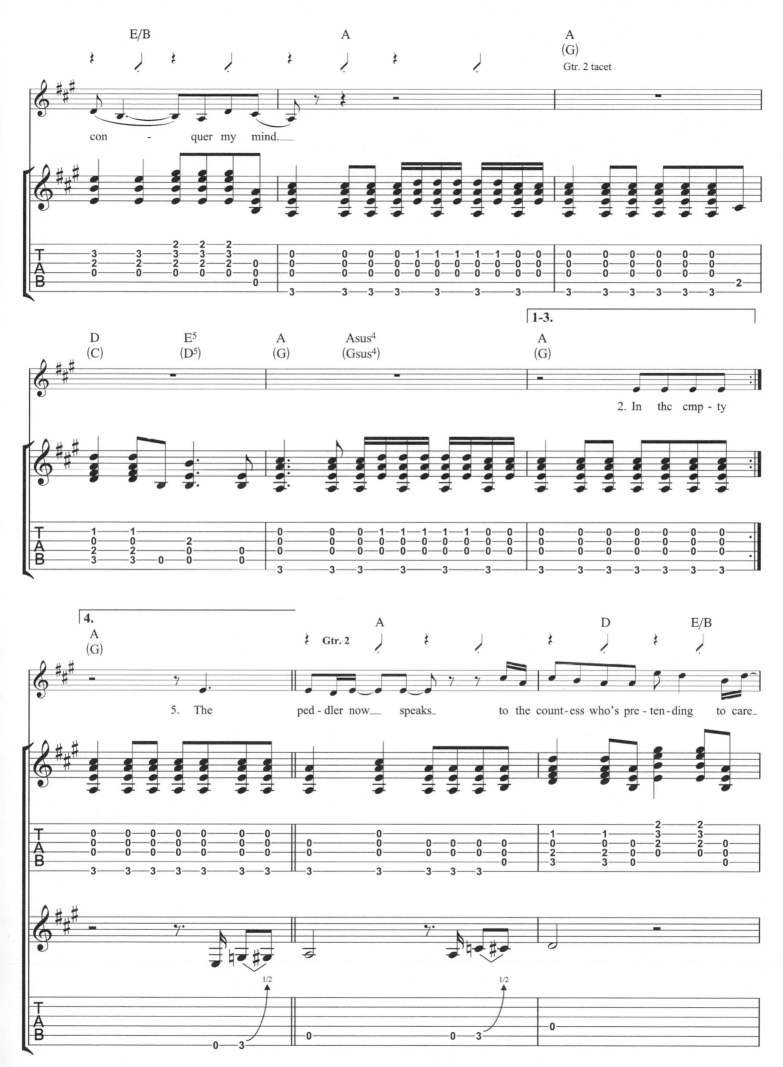

al-ways says___ "Ya can't look at much, can ya man?"as she,her-self,pre-pares___ for him.

And Ma-don-na, she still___ has not showed, we see this

empty cage now corrode where her cape of the stage once had flowed. The fiddler, he now steps to the road, He writes ev-'ry-

- thing's been re- turned___ which was owed___ on the back___ of the fish truck that loads___

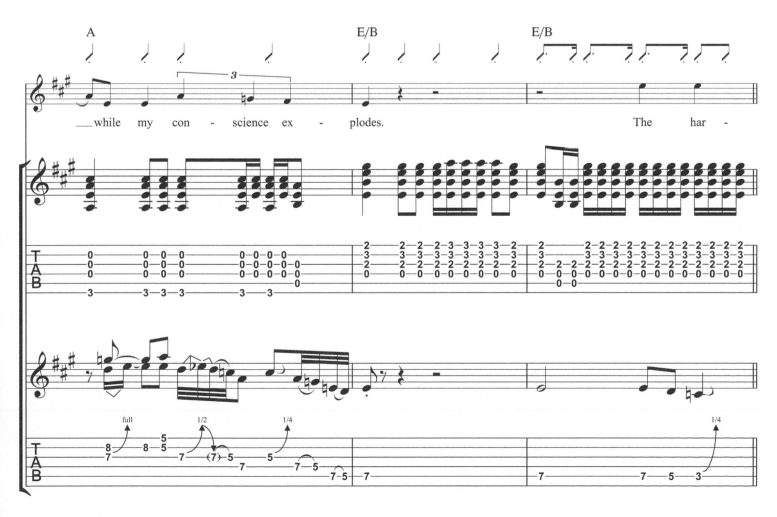

___ while my con - science ex - plodes. The har -

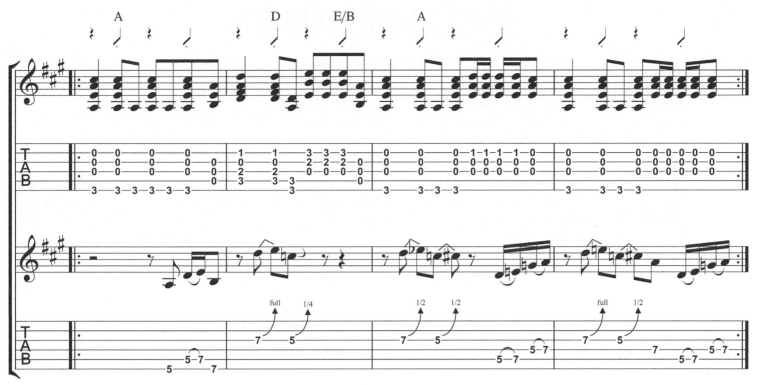

*Verse 2:*

In the empty lot where the ladies play blindman's buff with the key chain
And the all-night girls they whisper of escapades out on the "D" train
We can hear the night watchman click his flashlight
Ask himself if it's him or them that's really insane
Louise, she's all right, she's just near
She's delicate and seems like the mirror
But she just makes it all too concise and too clear
That Johanna's not here
The ghost of 'lectricity howls in the bones of her face
Where these visions of Johanna have now taken my place

*Verse 3:*

Now, little boy lost, he takes himself so seriously
He brags of his misery, he likes to live dangerously
And when bringing her name up
He speaks of a farewell kiss to me
He's sure got a lotta gall to be so useless and all
Muttering small talk at the wall while I'm in the hall
How can I explain?
Oh, it's so hard to get on
And these visions of Johanna, they keep me up past the dawn

*Verse 4:*

Inside the museums, Infinity goes up on trial
Voices echo this is what salvation must be like after a while
But Mona Lisa musta had the highway blues
You can tell by the way she smiles
See the primitive wallflower freeze
When the jelly-faced women all sneeze
Hear the one with the mustache say, "Jeeze
I can't find my knees"
Oh, jewels and binoculars hang from the head of the mule
But these visions of Johanna, they make it all seem so cruel

# YOU'RE A BIG GIRL NOW

Words & Music by Bob Dylan

in the rain, oh, oh, and you are on dry land.

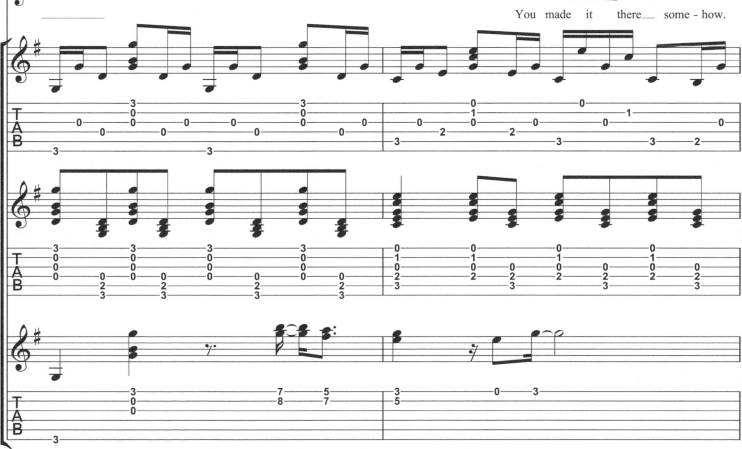

You made it there some - how.

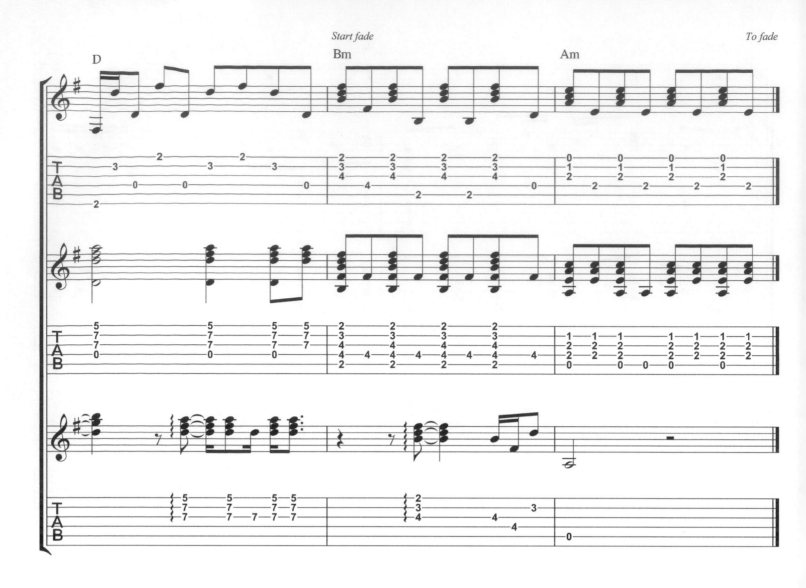

*Verse 3:*

Time is a jet plane, it moves too fast

Oh, but what a shame if all we've shared can't last

I can change, I swear, oh, oh

See what you can do

I can make it through

You can make it too

*Verse 4:*

Love is so simple, to quote a phrase

You've known it all the time, I'm learnin' it these days

Oh, I know where I can find you, oh, oh

In somebody's room

It's a price I have to pay

You're a big girl all the way

*Verse 5:*

A change in the weather is known to be extreme

But what's the sense of changing horses in midstream?

I'm going out of my mind, oh, oh

With a pain that stops and starts

Like a corkscrew to my heart

Ever since we've been apart